TOWN AND COUNTRY IN ROMAN BRITAIN

Archaeology

Editor
DR JOHN COLES
PH.D., M.A.
Lecturer in Archaeology in the
University of Cambridge

Watts Wells, Ditchley, from the air, looking north-east
(pp.111-2).   Note the smaller, and possibly earlier, complex
outside the south-west angle of the Roman enclosure.

Photograph by G. W. G. Allen   *By courtesy of the Ashmolean Museum*

TOWN AND COUNTRY
IN ROMAN BRITAIN

A. L. F. Rivet
MA, FSA

Reader in Romano-British Studies
in the University of Keele

HUTCHINSON UNIVERSITY LIBRARY
LONDON

HUTCHINSON & CO *(Publishers)* LTD
178–202 Great Portland Street, London W1

London Melbourne Sydney
Auckland Johannesburg Cape Town

First published 1958
Second edition 1964
Reprinted 1966, 1968, 1970

The map of Roman Silchester on the cover of the paperback edition is by courtesy of the Ordnance Survey and Reading Museum

Printed in Great Britain by litho on smooth wove paper by Anchor Press, and bound by Wm. Brendon, both of Tiptree, Essex

ISBN 09 045541 X (cased)
09 045542 8 (paper)

IN MEMORIAM

A. R. R.

1879–1955

CONTENTS

ILLUSTRATIONS

NOTE ON MAPS

The political map of Roman Britain (fig. 9) is intended only to illustrate the political divisions of the province. For a general map the reader is advised to refer throughout to the *Ordnance Survey Map of Roman Britain* (3rd edn., 1956).

Comme le champ semé en verdure foisonne,
De verdure se hausse en tuyau verdissant,
Du tuyau se hérisse en épi florissant,
D'épi jauni en grain, que le chaud assaisonne;

Et comme en la saison le rustique moissonne
Les ondoyants cheveux du sillon blondissant,
Les met d'ordre en javelle, et du blé jaunissant
Sur le champ dépouillé mille gerbes façonne:

Ainsi de peu à peu crut l'empire romain,
Tant qu'il fut dépouillé par la barbare main,
Qui ne laissa de lui que ces marques antiques

Que chacun va pillant, comme on voit le glaneur,
Cheminant pas à pas, recueillir les reliques
De ce qui va tombant après le moissonneur.

JOACHIM DU BELLAY

PREFACE

Although this is not a book for the expert, neither is it designed as an introduction to Roman Britain as a whole. Its scope is too narrow for that, for it is concerned only with the civil side of the province and important military developments here receive no more than a passing mention; and even within this restricted field some aspects of life, notably religion and art, are barely touched on. The readers I have had especially in mind are the growing body of intelligent and energetic amateurs who attend summer schools and provide the labour force of innumerable excavations; whose interest in the subject has already been aroused and who have read general books on it; but who wish to enquire further why certain views are held and how their own work fits into the pattern.

For this reason, while not eschewing conjecture, I have tried to relate each statement or suggestion to the evidence on which it depends. This has involved the inclusion of a cumbersome (though by no means comprehensive) bibliography. That is a necessity imposed by the nature of the subject, and the first step to be taken by anyone who wishes to look carefully into Roman Britain must be to join a national or local archaeological society which can provide adequate library facilities.

The bibliography, however, does not adequately reflect my debt to others. A work of this kind is bound to be nine-tenths compilation —'No news here; that which I have is stolen from others, *Dicitque mihi mea pagina, fur es.*' I wish to thank a number of friends with whom I have discussed various aspects of the subject and who have read and commented on parts of the book in typescript; and especially my editor, Professor C. F. C. Hawkes, for much advice, criticism and encouragement. I would also like to thank Mr. A. T. Chester for the care with which he has redrawn all my maps and plans.

For permission to reproduce or adapt copyright material my thanks are due to the Society of Antiquaries of London (figs. 6, 7 & 8), the Royal Archaeological Institute of Great Britain and Ireland (fig. 7), the Prehistoric Society (fig. 7) and the Ashmolean Museum (frontispiece); and for permission to quote from published works to the Cambridge University Press (publishers of *The Cambridge Mediaeval History*, quoted on page 29), the National Museum of Wales (*The Personality of Britain*, page 33) and Messrs. Methuen & Co. Ltd. (*The Archaeology of Roman Britain*, page 103). The outline plans of towns (figs. 2–5) are adapted from the six-inch Ordnance Survey maps (Crown copyright reserved) with the sanction of the Controller of H.M. Stationery Office. Finally, I am grateful to the Director General of the Ordnance Survey for permission to make use of the index of the Archaeology Division; the views and opinions expressed, however, are my own and in no sense official.

A. L. F. R.

Epsom, 1958

THE NATURE OF THE EVIDENCE

'We must consider how very little history there is: I mean real authentick history. That certain kings reigned and certain battles were fought, we can depend upon as true; but all the colouring, all the philosophy of history is conjecture.'

This pronouncement was directed at Gibbon, who was at the time engaged on *The Decline and Fall*. But, so Boswell tells us, he 'did not step forth in defence of that species of writing. He probably did not like to *trust* himself with Johnson.' And awful as the clash of giants would have been, it is the spectacle rather than the debate which we regret. It is the fashion now both to decry the colouring and philosophy of Gibbon and to question, if not the authenticity and reality, at least the significance of the kings and battles of Johnson. History today is economic and social first, and the contribution that can be made to it by archaeology, a source of information unknown to Johnson, is as acceptable as that of contemporary literature. Indeed, on a subject such as Roman Britain, and most of all on its civil aspect, where there is so much archaeology and so little literature, there is a temptation to regard the evidence revealed by the former as alone real and authentick and to dismiss that of the latter as colouring and philosophy.

This approach can rapidly lead to absurdity. The commonest form it takes is the presentation of Roman Britain as a fixed entity, suspended in time, and sometimes even in space. But historically 'Roman Britain' is a meaningless abstraction. Roman rule in Britain lasted for some four hundred years—about the same period as separates the reign of Elizabeth II from that of Elizabeth I—and while there was nothing comparable to the Industrial Revolution to transform it overnight it was a very different country in the fifth

century from what it had been in the first. Generations of archaeologists have given us an almost embarrassing wealth of information about it, but the arrangement of this material into some sort of
chronological and evolutionary order has scarcely begun. For such
an arrangement the essential framework can be provided only by
the authentick kings and battles. There are a number of questions
which archaeology can never answer, just as there are many subjects
on which literature is silent, and the recognition of this fact is so
fundamental that our enquiry can most profitably begin with a
review of the sources of our information.

The evidence on which our knowledge of Roman Britain is based
can conveniently be considered under five headings:

1. Literary Evidence.
2. Epigraphic Evidence.
3. Archaeological Evidence.
4. Evidence by Analogy.
5. The Opinions of Modern Scholars.

1. LITERARY EVIDENCE

There are references to Britain or the Britons in more than 120 of
the ancient authors. Collections or selections of them have been
made on several occasions, but while these are useful as reference
books they are subject to a number of shortcomings. In the first
place, the older ones do not conform to modern standards of palaeo-
graphy and textual criticism, so that the reading of any particular
passage needs to be checked against a later edition of the work
from which it is taken before any sound deductions can be made
from it. Secondly, they are in a sense too comprehensive, as many of
the entries consist of no more than poetical allusions to Ultima
Thule or the shores of Kent. Thirdly, they are, paradoxically, not
comprehensive enough, because their excerpts are too short.

In ancient Rome, history and biography, no less than oratory,
were cultivated arts, and a passage torn from its context can be
peculiarly misleading. For example, all the historians employ the
device of putting imaginary speeches into the mouths of prominent
men in moments of crisis. There is nothing intrinsically objection-
able in this, and indeed it was used by the greatest classical historian

of all. But whereas Thucydides was describing contemporary events and knew many of his speakers personally, it was not always so with the writers who refer to Roman Britain. It is debatable how much the speech which Tacitus puts into the mouth of Calgacus owed to information supplied by Agricola and how much to the historian's own cynical admiration for the noble savage; it is quite certain that the statements attributed to Boudicca by Cassius Dio (writing some 120 years later) reflect neither the state of British agriculture nor the powers of endurance of the Roman legionary in the first century.

But if Dio erred in his zeal to reconstruct the past, the opposite fault is the commoner. As we have already observed, there was nothing comparable to the Industrial Revolution in the ancient world and the same way of life, generally speaking, persisted from the foundation of Rome to the Middle Ages. Because there was so little of it, Roman writers were mostly blind to social change, even when it did occur. To Ammianus Marcellinus, writing in the fourth century, the times of Augustus (or of Alexander for that matter) were as intelligible as his own, and he saw the differences between them as moral rather than material. The Virgilian reference to Britain as 'a world apart' continues to appear right down to the fourth century, but while it may truly reflect the mental attitude of an inhabitant of Rome to the most distant province it has no more real significance than a reference to Sydney as an outpost of Empire; the local population would see it differently.

Thirdly, the Romans shared with the rest of mankind a tendency to note only the unusual in foreign countries and their inhabitants. This is displayed not only in encyclopaedists like Pliny, or deliberate collectors of the bizarre like Solinus, but also in many of the more serious writers. Here again we must remember the moral emphasis of Roman historiography and the absence of any scientific school of writing to balance it. The quantity of surviving references to Britain is not sufficient to justify a categorical statement on any particular point, but it is a reasonable supposition that where nothing is reported to the contrary the British way of life and thought did not differ fundamentally from the Gallic, or even the Italian, except that it was set in a lower key. A Virgilian couplet on a British mosaic pavement implies no more (and, of course, no less) affectation in its owner than a similar decoration in Italy.

With such considerations as these in mind—and they could be multiplied indefinitely—we may sum up the use of the literary evidence. As providing a basic framework of kings and battles it is essential; where references to Britain occur they need to be read strictly in their context; and while such references are all too few, the whole of Roman literature—history, biography, law, geography, agriculture, poetry even—is relevant. This amounts to saying that the wise student of Roman Britain will master the whole corpus of ancient writing—as Dr. Giles, in the preface to his collection, blandly remarks, 'To effect this object I have, in the first place, carefully gone through all the existing works of the Greek and Latin classics. . . .' For most of us this is an unattainable ideal, but it is worth remembering that it is an ideal, and that the archaeologist reading the classics is not wasting his time.

BIBLIOGRAPHY

The following is a selective list of the ancient literature bearing on Roman Britain; works of especial importance are indicated by the use of heavy type.

With regard to editions, those in the Oxford Classical Texts series (covering the 'classics' proper only) and those published by Teubner are reliable, but for the ordinary English reader the most convenient are probably those in the Loeb Library (published in England by Heinemann), which have a parallel text and translation; these are indicated by the letter (L). English translations of most of the 'classical' authors are included in the Everyman Library and in the rapidly growing Penguin Classics (P); translations of some of the others, such as Cassius Dio and Ammianus, were published in the now defunct Bohn Library, and can sometimes be found second-hand.

Authors marked with an asterisk (*) wrote in Greek, the remainder in Latin.

Collections

The standard collection is the Monumenta Historica Britannica (ed. Petrie and Sharpe, 1848). This included the texts of the literary passages which mention Britain, both Latin and Greek, with translations of the latter, and some inscriptions.

More manageable is J. A. Giles: *History of the Ancient Britons* (1847) in two volumes: the texts are in Vol. II, some translations and comments in Vol. I.

Both of these need to be used critically (see page 16 above). More recent and reliable is **R. W. Moore: The Romans in Britain** (Methuen, 1938). This contains a good selection of Latin texts, with notes, and a few translations (but not texts) from the Greek writers. It also has an excellent introduction and bibliography

History and Biography

Caesar (*d.* 44 B.C.): **De Bello Gallico** (L, P) is important not only for his own record of his British expeditions (IV: 20–8 and V: 8–23) but also for his account of Gaul and the Gauls, who were closely related to the Britons.

The History (L) of *Diodorus Siculus (*fl.* 30 B.C.) is chiefly of interest as preserving (V: 21–2) some of the account of Britain by Pytheas (*c.* 320 B.C.)

Tacitus (*d. c.* A.D. 118) wrote a history of Rome from the death of Augustus in A.D. 14 to the death of Domitian in 96. This was in two parts. The **Annals** (L, P) covered the period 14–68, but much of them has been lost, including the account of the Claudian invasion of Britain. The second period was dealt with in the **Histories** (L), which are in a still more fragmentary condition. So far as Britain is concerned, however, the loss is largely made good by the **Agricola** (L, P), Tacitus' biography of his father-in-law, Governor of Britain from 78 to 84, which includes a summary history of Roman Britain up to that date. The *Germania* (L, P) is useful as an account of barbarian life in the first century.

Suetonius (*d. c.* A.D. 140): *De Vita Caesarum,* the lives of the emperors from Julius Caesar to Domitian, is of incidental interest.

*Cassius Dio (*fl.* A.D. 230) wrote a **History** (L) from the foundation of Rome to A.D. 229. Much of it is lost, but among what survives is an account (LX: 19–23) of the Claudian invasion; and other references to Britain, including a passage (LXII: 1–4) dealing with the Boudiccan revolt, are preserved in an epitome of his work made by Xiphilinus in the eleventh century.

The **Historia Augusta** (L), a collection of lives by various hands of the emperors from Hadrian to Numerian (A.D. 117 to 284), would be of less importance if there were alternative sources for more of the period. The references to Britain are few and far between but sometimes vital.

*Herodian (*fl.* A.D. 240) wrote a **History** of the period from Marcus Aurelius to Gordian (A.D. 180 to 238). His references to Britain (II: 48–9 and III: 16–24 and 46–51) concern the Severan period (early third century).

Eutropius (*fl.* A.D. 365) wrote a short history of Rome from its foundation to the death of Jovian (A.D. 364). His only important reference to Britain (IX: 21–2) concerns the usurpation of Carausius.

For the end of the third and the beginning of the fourth century some information is provided by the Panegyrists, especially Eumenius (*fl.* A.D. 300) who has an account of Constantius' recovery of Britain from Allectus.

The last great Roman historian is **Ammianus Marcellinus** (*fl.* A.D. 380) whose **History** (L) was a not unworthy continuation of Tacitus. This included notes on the different provinces as they entered the narrative but that on Britain is unhappily among the many missing portions. Ammianus is of primary importance for the fourth century, not only for the scattered references to Britain but for the picture he gives of the contemporary state of affairs in Gaul and elsewhere.

Finally, there are several references to Britain in the History of *Zosimus (*fl.* A.D. 425), and for the sub-Roman period the *De Excidio Britanniae* of Gildas, a British Jeremiah of the early sixth century, is at least contemporary.

Geography

The *Geography of Strabo (*d. c.* A.D. 21) has references to Britain in Book I and a fuller account in Book IV and includes matter drawn from various sources ranging from Pytheas to Julius Caesar.

The *Geography of Ptolemy (*c.* A.D. 140) has an outline account of the geography of the British Isles expressed in terms of latitude and longitude. This is in Book II but needs to be studied in the light of the introductory Book I, which explains his aims and methods. The standard edition (ed. C. Muller, Paris 1883) has parallel Greek and Latin texts. A map of the British Isles compiled from Ptolemy's coordinates appears as fig. 1 in the introduction to the *Ordnance Survey Map of Roman Britain* (3rd edn., 1956).

Some geographical and other peculiarities of Britain, such as the absence of snakes in Thanet, are mentioned in the *Collectanea Rerum Memorabilium* of Solinus (*fl.* A.D. 200).

The **Antonine Itinerary** (*c.* A.D. 220, with later modifications) includes (sections 464–86) a number of routes in Britain ,with the mileages between places on them. The standard edition is that of O. Cuntz (*Itineraria Romana*, I, Leipzig, 1929); see also the *O.S. Map of Roman Britain* (3rd edn.) fig. 2.

The Peutinger Table is similar to the Antonine Itinerary in date and content but in the form of a schematic map. Of Britain only the southeast portion has survived and this is reproduced in *Antiquity*, I (1927), and in *Archaeologia*, XCIII (1949).

The **Notitia Dignitatum** (fourth century) is chiefly valuable for the military side of Britain, but has some particulars of the civil organisation too. The standard edition is that of O. Seeck (Berlin, 1876).

The **Ravenna Cosmography** (seventh century, but with no post-

Roman material) is a storehouse of geographical information which has, so far as Britain is concerned, been made intelligible by the edition of I. A. Richmond and O. G. S. Crawford, with philological notes by I. Williams, in *Archaeologia*, xciii (1949).

The *De Situ Britanniae* attributed to Richard of Cirencester is an eighteenth-century forgery which has confused the geography of Roman Britain since it was first imposed on Stukeley. Gibbon, though accepting it, remarked that Richard shows a knowledge of antiquity 'very extraordinary for a monk of the fourteenth century'. For a full and entertaining account of the matter see H. J. Randall's article 'Splendide Mendax' in *Antiquity*, vii (1933).

Miscellaneous

Important works on Roman agricultural practice, which bear on the romanisation of the British countryside, are **Varro** (*fl.* 30 B.C.): **Res Rusticae** and **Columella** (*fl.* A.D. 60): **De Re Rustica** (L).

The voluminous **Natural History** (L) of **Pliny the Elder** (*d.* A.D. 79) contains a number of references to Britain. Roman methods of land-surveying are described in the works (first to fifth century) collected under the title of *Gromatici Veteres*; there is an edition by Blume, Lachman and Rudorff (Berlin, 1848–52) but no English translation and they are largely untranslatable.

On buildings, building materials and mechanical devices, the *De Architectura* of Vitruvius (first century) is interesting; there is a good English translation by Warren (Harvard & O.U.P., 1914).

Roman law is a field of its own, best approached through modern works. The basic documents are the *Institutes of Gaius* (second century A.D.) and the *Digest* of Justinian (sixth century); for specific references to Britain see E. Birley: *Roman Britain and the Roman Army* (Titus Wilson, 1953), chap. V, and C. E. Stevens: 'A Possible Conflict of Laws in Roman Britain' (*Journal of Roman Studies*, xxxvii, 1947).

For poetry, **Virgil** (L, P) is, of course, uniquely important because of his enduring influence on Roman thought—exemplified in Britain by the couplet on the pavement in the Lullingstone villa and the Dido and Aeneas mosaic at Low Ham. Of more direct interest, however, are the Gaulish writers of the fourth century, whose thought cannot have been entirely different from that of their British contemporaries. A typical example is Ausonius (L). Gibbon remarked that 'the poetical fame of Ausonius condemns the taste of his age'; modern readers may find a more kindly introduction in the *Mediaeval Latin Lyrics* (P) of Helen Waddell, where Latin excerpts are paralleled by the best translations of poetry to be found anywhere. Also valuable on the literature of this period are N. K. Chadwick (ed.): *Studies in Early British History* (C.U.P., 1954) and N. K. Chadwick: *Poetry and Letters in Early Christian Gaul* (Bowes, 1955).

2. EPIGRAPHIC EVIDENCE

Inscriptions occupy a position midway between pure literature and pure archaeology. As written documents they are in a sense literary, as objects found on ancient sites they are archaeological, and the information they yield is of many kinds. The most spectacular of these is exemplified by the recent discovery of the inscription at Verulamium, which provided a close dating for the erection of the gateway to the forum, but humbler examples contribute their quota too. An inscribed milestone may not only indicate the date of road repairs and confirm the Roman name of a town, it may also tell us something about political geography. A religious dedication may give us both the identity of a local deity and the name and origin of one of his worshippers. And while an inscription to a reigning emperor is likely to reflect fashion rather than feeling, in funerary monuments, and still more in graffiti, we may sometimes gain an insight into human sentiment of a kind which we seek in vain in the more pretentious works of the historians. In the words of Collingwood, 'the value of inscriptions as historical material is so great that it can hardly be exaggerated', and their comparative scarcity in the civil part of Roman Britain renders them all the more precious.

While the finer points of epigraphy are a specialised subject, its general principles are not obscure and can be mastered by a study of published work combined with the inspection of examples in museums and elsewhere. It is, however, a study which needs to be pursued, if only by reading, beyond the bounds of Britain, for few inscriptions are recovered intact and comparative material from the whole of the Empire has to be taken into account. Given this, the texts of official and formal Roman inscriptions are so stereotyped that quite extensive restorations, if made by an experienced epigraphist, can be accepted without scepticism.

BIBLIOGRAPHY

The best English introduction to Latin epigraphy is chapter XI of Collingwood's *The Archaeology of Roman Britain* (Methuen, 1930). A fuller work is Cagnat: *Cours d'Épigraphie Latine* (Paris, 4th edn., 1914). This has no English equivalent, but especially valuable for the use to which inscriptions may be put is Birley: *Roman Britain and the Roman Army* (Titus Wilson, 1953), particularly chapter XIV.

The inscriptions of the whole Empire were collected in the *Corpus Inscriptionum Latinarum* (C.I.L.). Those from Britain are contained in Vol. VII (Berlin, 1873). This was edited by the German E. Hübner, whose knowledge of Britain was limited, and contains a number of errors, particularly of location. Additions and corrections were published in the now defunct periodical *Ephemeris Epigraphica* (E.E.), British sections appearing in Vols. III, IV, VII and IX (the last two by Haverfield). More were included in Haverfield: *Roman Britain in 1913* and *Roman Britain in 1914* (British Academy) and since 1921 they have appeared annually in the *Journal of Roman Studies*. A new collection, *The Roman Inscriptions of Britain*, has been in preparation for many years, and the first volume is expected shortly.

Dessau: *Inscriptiones Latinae Selectae* (I.L.S.) is a valuable classified selection, but is in fewer libraries than it should be, and difficult to obtain. A selection of British inscriptions is contained in A. R. Burn: *The Romans in Britain* (Blackwell, 1932) and also in R. W. Moore's book of the same title, already cited.

For language in Roman Britain, and especially Celtic names, see K. Jackson: *Language and History in Early Britain* (Oliver & Boyd, 1953), and Holder: *Alt-celtischer Sprachschatz* (Leipzig, 1896–1913).

3. ARCHAEOLOGICAL EVIDENCE

Archaeology provides so much of our material that an understanding of the technique of excavation—its limitations as well as its capabilities—is essential to the study of Roman Britain. Such an understanding can only be acquired by experience, but while there is some truth in the saying that excavation is simply commonsense it does not follow that each generation of excavators must set out in the light of commonsense alone. Moreover excavation is by its very nature destructive, and Roman Britain is not the bottomless bran tub that it once appeared to be. The nineteenth-century trail of evidence destroyed and questions unanswered (and now often unanswerable) makes sorry reading. In most cases the damage was done because two simple principles were not understood—the principle of stratification and the principle of the 'ghost wall'. Both of these are indeed 'commonsense', but we must in honesty wonder what principles which will appear in the same light to our successors are being overlooked today. The beginner will best serve both himself and posterity by learning from the expert rather than by launching out on his own.

Excavation, however, is not the only form of archaeology. A great deal of evidence has been accumulated by inspection on the ground and from the air, without ever a spade being put into the earth. This is obviously so in the case of roads and military earthworks, but field archaeology has other uses too. The course of a town ditch, long filled, may be revealed by settlement-cracks in modern buildings; the names of fields, like Blacklands or Sunken Church Field or Chessels (=small stones, often tesserae) may point to new Roman sites; field systems leave their traces on the ground and are visible still more widely on air photographs; and chance finds of pottery and tiles and coins may transform our conception of the degree of romanisation attained in a given area in a given period. Information obtained in this way is no less important than that got from excavation and involves no destruction of evidence.

The identification and classification of the objects themselves is another essential activity of archaeology, and the degree of their reliability, or unreliability, as precise dating material needs to be appreciated. For example, fine pottery, like Samian, tends to be less wantonly discarded, and so to have a longer life, than coarse pottery; and even coins, the best dating objects of all, have survival patterns peculiar to the various issues. All these and several others—jewellery, furniture, wall plaster, mosaic pavements—are subjects of specialised study.

Nevertheless it is only in its content, whether buildings or small objects, and not in its technique, that Romano-British archaeology differs from prehistoric or mediaeval archaeology, or any archaeology whatsoever. And the Romano-British archaeologist cannot afford to be too much of a specialist. This is most obvious in the field: you cannot identify a Roman barrow if you do not know what Bronze Age barrows, and mediaeval mottes, look like, and villages deserted in the Middle Ages are still from time to time wrongly identified as 'Roman towns'. The archaeologist, and especially the field archaeologist, must know what to reject as well as what to accept. Above all, Roman Britain is only one phase of British history

which, however *disiecta* its surviving *membra*, was, and is, a continuous process. The story of Roman Britain begins in the Early
Iron Age and ends in the Dark Ages, and anyone who tries to understand it without reference to these two periods at least is doomed to
frustration.

BIBLIOGRAPHY

The best statement of the aims and methods of archaeology in general
is Wheeler: *Archaeology from the Earth* (O.U.P., 1954, Penguin, 1956),
and for field archaeology (as distinct from digging) Crawford: *Archaeology
in the Field* (Phoenix House, 1953) is invaluable; the latter includes an
excellent bibliography. Webster: *Practical Archaeology* (Black, 1963) is a
useful practical guide. Excavations at which volunteers are welcome are
listed in the *Calendar of Excavations* issued by the Council for British
Archaeology, 8 St. Andrews Place, London, N.W.10.

On Romano-British archaeology the standard work is Collingwood:
The Archaeology of Roman Britain (Methuen, 1930). This is out of print
and to a certain extent out of date, but apart from the chapters on 'villages'
and on coarse pottery is still generally reliable. The geographical distribution of Roman sites is shown on the *Ordnance Survey Map of Roman
Britain* (3rd edn., 1956).

For details of individual sites the best starting point is the *Victoria
History of the Counties of England* (V.C.H.). Sections dealing with the
Roman period have been published for twenty-six counties, but while they
are all useful as lists of discoveries the value of their interpretations varies,
and they may be roughly classified as follows:

(1) Those by the late Professor F. Haverfield, viz. Derby (I, 1905),
Hants (I, 1900), Norfolk (I, 1901), Northants (I, 1902), Salop (I, 1908),
Somerset (I, 1906), Warwick (I, 1904), Worcs (I, 1901).

(2) Those which maintain Haverfield's standard, viz. Cornwall (Part 5,
1924), Hunts (I, 1926), Kent (III, 1932), Oxon (I, 1939), Wilts (I (i) 1957—
list only, discussion forthcoming), Essex (III, 1963).

(3) Others, viz. Beds (III, 1908), Berks (I, 1906), Bucks (II, 1908),
Hereford (I, 1908), Herts (IV, 1914), Leics (I, 1907), Notts (II, 1910),
Rutland (I, 1908), Staffs (I, 1908), Suffolk (I, 1911), Surrey (IV, 1912),
Sussex (III, 1935).

The *V.C.H.* of London is not included in the above list because it is
entirely superseded by the Royal Commission on Historical Monuments volume *Roman London* (1928), which is exhaustive up to its date of
publication.

For the period implied in its title all important new discoveries are mentioned, with references, in Kendrick and Hawkes: *Archaeology in England and Wales, 1914–31* (Methuen, 1932, out of print). Volumes on the counties of Berkshire, Cornwall, Kent, Middlesex, Somerset, Surrey, Sussex and Yorkshire, also with references, were published by Methuen in the 1930's, but only Sussex, of which a second edition appea red in 1954, is now in print. To these may be added Grinsell: *The Archaeology of Wessex* (Methuen, 1958), Kitson Clark: *A Gazetteer of Roman Remains in the East Riding of Yorkshire* (Yorks Archaeological Society, 1935), and Phillips: 'The Present State of Archaeology in Lincolnshire' (*Archaeological Journal* xc, 1933, and xci, 1934).

Romano-British sites discovered from the air are recorded and interpreted, with useful bibliographical notes, in J. K. St. Joseph's periodical surveys under the title of 'Air Reconnaissance of Britain', published in the *Journal of Roman Studies* from Volume xli (1951) onwards. On air photography in general, see J. S. P. Bradford: *Ancient Landscapes* (Bell, 1957).

When using reference books such as the *V.C.H.* (and especially those in category 3) it is generally advisable to refer back to the original excavation reports. A few of these have been published as separate books, but they normally appear in the journals of the national or county archaeological societies. The most important national journals in this context are *The Journal of Roman Studies, The Antiquaries Journal, The Archaeological Journal, The Journal of the British Archaeological Association, Archaeologia Cambrensis, The Bulletin of the Board of Celtic Studies* and the *Proceedings of the Society of Antiquaries of Scotland*. For county and regional journals, see the bibliography to chapter 6.

Special Subjects (supplementary to Collingwood).

For coins, the standard work of reference is Mattingly and Sydenham: *The Roman Imperial Coinage* (i–v, ix, Spink, 1923–51). For their use as evidence see also Sutherland: *Coinage and Currency in Roman Britain* (O.U.P., 1937) and O'Neil: 'Coins and Archaeology' (*Archaeological Journal*, xcii (1935), 64 *ff.*). A cheap and useful hand-list is *A Catalogue of Roman Coins* (B. A. Seaby, 1948).

For coarse pottery there is as yet no general work, although in the north a firm foundation has been laid by J. P. Gillam's article 'Types of Roman Coarse Pottery in Northern Britain' (*Archaeologia Aeliana* (4th series), xxxv (1957)). In the south recourse must be had to recent excavation reports in which this class of find is fully dealt with. Especially important are the Reports of the Research Committee of the Society of Antiquaries XIV (*Camulodunum*), XV (*The Jewry Wall, Leicester*), XX (*Roman Colchester*) and XXI (*The Roman Potters' Kilns of Colchester*).

For roads, the standard work is now Margary: *Roman Roads in Britain* (2 vols., Phoenix House, 1955 and 1957). Liversidge: *Furniture in Roman Britain* (Tiranti, 1955) is a useful book on a neglected subject.

4. EVIDENCE BY ANALOGY

Since Roman Britain formed part of a world empire, and one moreover in which it was deliberate policy to assimilate the provinces to the ways of life and government of the centre, it follows that our knowledge of the other provinces can amplify and illumine what we know of Britain.

Unfortunately those parts of the Empire which are most fully documented, Italy and the East, are not closely comparable with Britain and analogy from them needs to be used with particular caution. But there is a great deal of information on the other Celtic provinces, and especially Gaul, which is immediately relevant. Much of it is derived from literary and epigraphic sources, but even in archaeology, although excavation, and still more fieldwork, has sometimes fallen below British standards, Gaul has the advantage of a much greater wealth of extant structures. On the Celtic side proper, there is vital information still to be gathered from those areas which were not directly affected by Roman rule, especially from Ireland.

Nor is analogy necessarily restricted to the time at which the Roman Empire flourished. Throughout history contacts between higher and lower civilisations have tended to follow set patterns, and our understanding of the earlier stages of the romanisation of Britain can be deepened by the study of such processes as the westernisation of Africa in the last hundred years. There are, of course, important differences—for example, the Romans never became involved in the futility of race and colour prejudice—but the similarities, both general and particular, are sometimes startling. As with contemporary analogy, this cannot add to our knowledge; it is not, in the strictest sense, evidence of fact. But it is evidence of feeling, it can point to probabilities, and it can confirm us in some of the conclusions we may reach by other means.

BIBLIOGRAPHY

An excellent English introduction to Gaul is Brogan: *Roman Gaul* (Bell, 1953), which includes a comprehensive bibliography. The standard French work is Grenier: *Archéologie Gallo-Romaine* (4 volumes in 7 parts, Paris, 1931–1960), while the books by H-P. Eydoux in the series *D'un Monde à l'autre* (Plon) contain popular accounts of a very high standard of recent excavations. Cumont: *Comment la Belgique fut Romanisée* (2nd edn., Brussels, 1920) is still, despite its age, a most stimulating review of Gallia Belgica. Belgian villas are covered by de Maeyer: *De Romeinsche Villa's in België* (Antwerp, 1937), which is in Flemish but has a French summary and plenty of plans. For Gaulish sculpture, which frequently portrays scenes of everyday life, the standard collection is Espérandieu: *Recueil Général des Bas-reliefs, Statues et Bustes de la Gaule Romaine* (twelve volumes and supplements, Paris, 1907 onwards).

There is no satisfactory map of Roman Gaul. Sheet L.31 (Lugdunum) (Paris, 1935) of the *Tabula Imperii Romani* covers the area around and west of Lyons, and Sheet M.32 (Moguntiacum) (Frankfurt, 1940) part of the eastern edge of the province. Some départements have been treated in the series *Forma Orbis Romani*, but its approach is bibliographical rather than cartographical.

On Spain there is now Wiseman: *Roman Spain* (Bell, 1956). For other Celtic provinces, such as Raetia and Noricum, and the rest of the Empire see Vols. x, xi and xii of the *Cambridge Ancient History*.

For modern analogies it will suffice to mention Hailey: *An African Survey* (O.U.P., 1938, 2nd edn., 1957), which is a storehouse of information on the social and administrative problems that arise in the early stages of the assimilation of backward societies to a more developed culture and on the various ways—some of them very similar to those adopted by the Romans—in which they have been attacked.

5. THE OPINIONS OF MODERN SCHOLARS

Here indeed we come to the conjecture and the colouring and the philosophy, and very rewarding they can be. But the listing of them as a form of evidence implies also the responsibility to treat them as rigorously as its other forms. In assessing their value two distinct judgements have to be made, the one psychological, concerning the historical sense of the author, the other technical, to determine how much of the primary evidence has been taken into account. The first of these hardly admits of discussion, but the second requires some comment. As has already been suggested, the new evidence, derived from archaeology, is an addition to, not a replacement of, the old evidence, derived from literature. A capable archaeologist is not necessarily a good historian and muddy boots must sometimes be changed for slippers, the windy hilltop for the library ladder. It is still possible to read Gibbon for profit as well as for pleasure because, though totally ignorant of archaeology in the modern sense, he had an unrivalled knowledge of the literature. While it is obvious that the latest book is potentially the best, because new evidence is always coming to light, the potentiality is not always fulfilled.

That there are bad books as well as good books on Roman Britain hardly needs saying. With regard to the former, one cannot do better than recall what Haverfield wrote in 1911:

'The student needs to be warned that the literature of Roman Britain contains a larger proportion than the literature of any other historical subject of unsound and unscholarly work. Much of this is valuable as a record of finds but the interpretation of the finds and the theories based on them are too often worthless, even when they seem to be authoritative.'

With regard to the good books, one curious feature of Romano-British studies must be noted. This is the tendency, perhaps due to the intractable nature of the evidence, to create myths. For example, the nineteenth-century picture of Britain was of a land of forts and sumptuous villas inhabited by 'rich Romans' (usually generals) on the one hand, and seething masses of savage blue-painted Britons on the other. Haverfield corrected this impression, pointing out that Briton and Roman were not mutually exclusive terms and that in fact most of the Roman civilisation had a British content. But this has resulted, through no fault of Haverfield's, in the new myth, admittedly less harmful than the old, of a province so thoroughly British that no foreign landowner would dare to show his face in it. Haverfield, again, produced the concept of military and civil zones in Britain. This was, and is, a most valuable aid to the understanding of the province, but it has given rise to the myth of a land in which all civil life was located in the south-east and all military forces in the north and west; so that the existence of a stone-built fort in London comes as a surprise and the civilised life of the settlements attached to many of the northern forts appears somehow abnormal. Thirdly, Collingwood drew a distinction between villas on the one hand and villages on the other and, quite logically (given his premisses), evolved the idea of two forms of social organisation existing side by side. More recent archaeological work has indicated that most of Collingwood's villages were in fact single farms and thus his argument is undermined at its base. But the myth persists and the term 'village' is still too widely used, with all its misleading implications.

These three examples by no means exhaust the tale of Romano-British myths, but they suffice to point the moral. This is that any summary account, from however eminent a pen, must be measured carefully against the evidence. Much of what is written about Roman Britain must, in the nature of things, be hypothetical, and as hypothesis it must be treated; finality is still a long way off.

BIBLIOGRAPHY
The Roman Empire
The best general work, which also has a thoroughly comprehensive bibliography, is the *Cambridge Ancient History* (C.U.P.). The volumes which are immediately relevant are:
    Vol. X (1934) for the period 44 B.C. to A.D. 70.
    Vol. XI (1936) for A.D. 70 to 192.
    Vol. XII (1939) for A.D. 193 to 324.
    The fourth century is covered by Vol. I of the *Cambridge Mediaeva. History* (1911), but many of its conclusions require modification in the light of more recent evidence and the usefulness of its bibliography is restricted by its age.
    Rostovtzeff: *Social and Economic History of the Roman Empire* (O.U.P., 1926, 2nd edn., revised by P. M. Fraser, 1958) contains a mass of valuable material and Vol. III of Tenney Frank (ed): *Economic Survey of Rome* (Johns Hopkins Press, Baltimore, 1937) includes sections on Britain by Collingwood, on Gaul by Grenier and on Spain by Van Nostrand.
    An English translation of Carcopino: *Daily Life in Ancient Rome* has now (1956) been published as a Pelican and provides a good account of the life towards which the provincial centres, however slowly and unwittingly, were tending.

Encyclopaedias and Dictionaries
The standard work of reference is the German Pauly-Wissowa: *Realencyclopädie der Classischen Altertumswissenschaft* (approximately 30 volumes and supplements, Stuttgart, 1894 onwards). In view of the period

over which its publication has been spread some articles must be treated with reserve, but it is a monument of scholarship and its bibliography is invaluable. Somewhat smaller, but also extremely useful, is the French Daremberg and Saglio: *Dictionnaire des Antiquités Grecques et Romaines* (5 volumes, Paris, 1877–1919). The nearest English equivalent to these works is the one-volume *Oxford Classical Dictionary* (O.U.P., 1949); this is good on subjects which lie on or near the highroad of history, but disappointing on the byways.

Roman Britain

The best general work is I. A. Richmond: *Roman Britain* (Vol. I in the *Pelican History of England*, 2nd edn., 1963). This is available both bound and paper-backed and is indispensable to any student of Roman Britain.

Among earlier works which may still be read with profit, especial mention must be made of two by F. Haverfield: *Roman Britain* (ed. G. Macdonald. O.U.P., 1923) and *The Romanisation of Roman Britain* (4th edn., ed. G. Macdonald, O.U.P., 1923), and two by R. G. Collingwood: *Roman Britain* (O.U.P., 2nd edn., 1934) and (with J. N. L. Myres) *Roman Britain and the English Settlements* (O.U.P., 2nd edn., 1937); the latter is the larger work and, as it is more detailed, has suffered more from the march of archaeology, but it is still among the masterpieces of English historical writing. The scope of E. Birley's *Roman Britain and the Roman Army* (Titus Wilson, 1953) is wider than its title suggests and it may properly be mentioned here, as may also A. R. Burn: *Agricola and Roman Britain* (E.U.P., 1953) and M. P. Charlesworth: *The Lost Province, or The Worth of Britain* (University of Wales, 1949).

Essays on various aspects of Roman Britain appear from time to time in the *Journal of Roman Studies*, in *Antiquity* and in the *English Historical Review*, and occasionally in the other national journals mentioned in the last section.

.   .   .   .   .

From what has been said it will be evident that our knowledge of Roman Britain is not to be compared with a firmly founded building to which each new discovery adds a brick. A juster comparison would be with a jigsaw puzzle. We know the sort of picture that should emerge because, although our own key plan is torn and faded almost beyond recognition, the plans of some other puzzles in the same series are in rather better condition. The fact that the others were made on the same jig also helps us, though we realise that this was modified from time to time while the series was in production. Of the pieces of our own puzzle, some have fallen in the fire, some have been chewed by the dog and yet others have been trimmed to fit where they do not really belong. We shall never recover the whole picture. But the nearer we get to it the clearer will be our understanding not of Roman Britain only but of the whole Empire of which it formed a part.

THE CELTIC BACKGROUND

Though the people of Britain at the time of its absorption into the Roman Empire were not naked savages, neither were they in any way the equals of their conquerors. This is especially true of their standard of social and political competence and because of it the distribution and character of human occupation generally present a reaction to, rather than a dominance over, what Sir Cyril Fox has called the Personality of Britain. The settlement pattern was that of a primitive society, depending almost entirely on natural circumstances. The essentials were security against man and beast and the availability and accessibility of productive land. These in turn were determined by the relationship of natural forests and parkland and the existence of natural lines of communication, that is to say ridgeways and rivers. Man was the suppliant, not yet the master, of nature.

Here we are concerned primarily with the lowland zone which, as Fox points out, 'is easily overrun by invaders, and on it new cultures of continental origin brought across the narrow seas tend to be imposed'. The prehistory of lowland Britain is a long tale of wave after wave of immigrants sometimes surging, sometimes trickling, across the Channel, and the story of the people whom the Romans called Britons has thus no clear beginning. Further, 'the ultimate expression of any continental culture in Lowland Britain tends to possess individual characters. The sea barrier inhibits mass movement and encourages independent adventure; lowland culture at any given period thus tends to represent the mingling of diverse continental elements rather than the extension beyond the Straits of a single continental culture'. So while each phase of British prehistory can only be dated and its origins understood by reference to the continent, it can never be satisfactorily described in continental terms. For this reason, in dealing with the prehistoric Iron Age,

British archaeologists now use the letters A, B and C to designate the broad cultural divisions, rather than the continental terms Hallstatt and La Tène.

This scheme was first propounded by Professor Hawkes in 1930 and although a number of refinements have been introduced since then, some of them by Hawkes himself, the main distinctions still hold good. Its use has transformed our understanding of a very complex period of history, but one point regarding it needs to be stressed at the outset. A, B and C are not chronological terms. A comes on the scene before B, and B before C, it is true, but A also persists, sometimes with no external modification, right down to the Roman period, and there are large areas not affected by C. Thus, though it is possible to refer to 'Iron Age B times' when speaking of the sequence at a particular site (at Maiden Castle, for instance), the same phrase applied to the country as a whole is meaningless. Nor are they linguistic or tribal terms. So far as can be deduced (mainly from the names of persons and places) all our Iron Age immigrants were Brythonic-speaking Celts, but we do not know how far the earlier peoples were grouped in tribes and most of the later tribes, with whom the Romans had to deal, were compounded of elements drawn from all three cultures. These terms are *cultural*, in the sense that although the manifestations of each group vary from place to place and develop in time, there are yet enough common factors which can be recognized in their way of life, their pottery and other gear, and their disposal of the dead, to distinguish A from B and B from C.

It is not possible to give a firm date for the arrival of the first iron-using people in Britain, not only because we are still in deep prehistory but also because they evidently came as part of a movement which had already begun in the Late Bronze Age. This continuity is perhaps clearest in Sussex, on such sites as Park Brow, but elsewhere on some of the earliest Iron Age sites, like Fengate (Peterborough) and Standlake, in Oxfordshire, there is continued use not only of living areas but of cemeteries too. The movement was due to pressure on France and the Low Countries from tribes lying further east, and since our iron-users evidently left their continental homes at about the time the Hallstatt phase of culture was giving way to that of La Tène, a starting date in the early fifth century would not be

far wide of the mark. This applies to the first culture which we call
Iron Age A. To begin with, the people concerned were mostly peace-
ful agriculturalists and their typical settlements were undefended. It
was in no sense an organised invasion but rather the infiltration of
small groups, who were themselves refugees, and it continued for
many years. The groups had, however, a common origin, in that
they all derived from various places lying between Normandy and
the Rhine. Gradually they spread over the area of primary settlement in south and east Britain, moving up the river valleys and along
the ridgeways, and apart from some backward areas of Wales and
the north, where the Bronze Age stock appears to have been very
little diluted, came to form the basis of the country's population not
only in the Iron Age but in the Roman period too.

In time, however, as the established groups developed and as
more joined them, a change came over their culture which in some
areas is sufficiently marked to justify its definition archaeologically
as Iron Second A. Here again a precise date can obviously not be
given, but 350 B.C. is a reasonable approximation. The change is
marked by developments in their pottery and other possessions, but
it is also in this phase that the building of hill forts begins in earnest.
The farmstead ringed by a palisade or light earthwork develops
first into a substantially defended enclosure and then into a full-
scale fortification. In the south most of this military activity appears
to date from about now and to represent a reaction to an
external threat.

The threat came from the bearers of our second culture-complex,
to which we give the name of Iron Age B. These people came mostly
from the part of France extending from Brittany to the Marne basin,
in which the La Tène culture was by now firmly established. As with
their predecessors, their movements were spread over a large area
and a long period of time, and their effect on Britain varied greatly
from region to region. In Cornwall, where they probably arrived
earliest, seeking tin, and where a Spanish element is also discernible,
they settled in some numbers and from there spread up the Bristol
Channel into Somerset, where they founded the Glastonbury lake
villages, up the Severn into South Wales, and along the Jurassic
Way as far as Hunsbury in Northampton. In Yorkshire a separate
group were responsible for the Arras culture, with its characteristic

chariot burials. In Wessex and Sussex their first incursions seem to have been little more than raids, but they left behind them pockets of influence which gave rise to a cultural phase we call AB, characterised by improved techniques in weaving and pottery-making and by the introduction of rotary querns to replace the saddle querns hitherto used for grinding corn. Finally further movements of people carrying a variant of the B culture took place in the first century B.C. particularly after Caesar's conquest of Gaul, into Wessex and Sussex. It was apparently these B peoples who introduced, or evolved, the system of multiple defences for hill forts and who provided the aristocracy of those tribes of southern Britain which did not fall completely under Belgic domination.

The Belgae themselves form the third cultural group, Iron Age C. Their influence, too, takes the form both of a folk movement and a domination. The folk movement began about 100 B.C. when some elements of the Belgic tribes, who lived in eastern France and Belgium, crossed over into Britain and established themselves first in Kent, then in Hertfordshire and Essex, where they emerge into history as the Catuvellauni. From here they extended their power, first eastwards into the territory of the Trinovantes, where they established their new capital of Camulodunum, and finally, under King Cunobelin in the first half of the first century A.D., over the greater part of south-east Britain. Before this, however, about 50 B.C., again as a result of Caesar's conquests, a further group of Belgae, under the leadership of Commius, the Atrebatic chief who was alternately the agent and the enemy of Caesar, had crossed into Britain and set up a kingdom in the area between the middle Thames and the coasts of Hampshire and West Sussex. The approximate extent of this kingdom is indicated by the distribution of coins inscribed with the names of Commius' descendants, but its precise character, in cultural terms, is still obscure. It is, however, clear that from the first the Atrebatic kingdom, as compared with the Catuvellaunian, incorporated a higher proportion of the earlier, non-Belgic, stock, and this applies still more to those areas, in Wiltshire and the upper Thames valley, where other Belgic groups settled. But the sequence of these movements is not absolutely clear and it has indeed been suggested that there were Atrebatic settlers in the middle Thames area before Commius crossed over.

Almost the whole of this picture is derived from archaeological sources. The knowledge which the literate world had of Britain before the expeditions of Julius Caesar was derived from the writings of Pytheas, a Greek merchant of Marseille, who visited the country about 320 B.C. Most of the ancient writers regarded Pytheas as a liar, but they quoted him nonetheless, and although it is not always clear when they are doing so, his account seems to have noted the following. He described the export of tin from Cornwall, which he called Belerium, and mentioned several geographical peculiarities, notably the tides (thereby, incidentally, establishing his *bona fides*). The people were numerous and under many chiefs, who used chariots in warfare, though they generally lived at peace with one another; the inhabitants of Belerium were particularly hospitable. Dwellings were of wood and thatch and the people were simple in their ways. They stored grain in roofed or underground structures, grinding it as they required it. In some parts they threshed it indoors, and those who had both corn and honey brewed a drink from them.

These scraps of information, all derived from quotations by much later authors, indicate that the full text of Pytheas' account would tell us more about the earlier phase of the British Iron Age than any number of excavations. In the meantime, however, we can supplement him with information gathered in this way from a number of sites. The fullest picture is derived from the farmstead at Little Woodbury, near Salisbury, which was excavated by Dr. Bersu in 1938. Here a circular occupation area of more than three acres was enclosed by a palisade and, for a brief period only, a ring ditch (the latter was never completed). Inside were the post-holes and other indications of a circular dwelling-house, fifty feet in diameter; one other similar but smaller building; a number of shallow hollows; and a very large number of pits and postholes. These pits have been noted on many sites dated to the Iron Age and to the Roman period not only in Wessex but over much of south-east Britain too, and in the past they have sometimes been described as pit dwellings. The details of their construction, the condition of their sides, and their siting in relation to other structures and to each other, as revealed at Little Woodbury, finally exploded this inter-pretation. The character of their filling showed that most of them were not in origin rubbish pits, and the absence of a durable lining ruled out their use as cisterns. They were, in fact, storage pits, chiefly for grain. Among the postholes, although over a large area they made a maze which could not be disentangled, two kinds of structure could be distinguished. One, represented by a square arrangement of holes, was interpreted as granaries, the other, represented by a pair of holes only, as drying racks for corn and hay.

The procedure implied by the presence of both underground storage pits and overground granaries is somewhat as follows. After harvesting the corn was divided into two parts, one for consumption, and one for seed. That for consumption was parched to improve its keeping qualities, in primitive ovens made of cob, fragments of which were discovered and whose use also explained the large quantity of ash and burnt flints (so-called pot-boilers) found on the site. This corn was then stored in the pits, which would have their covers sealed with clay against the wet. Nevertheless, even with such a covering, and despite the fact that they must have been lined with wickerwork or skins, the constant use of the pits would tend to produce mould and their frequent renewal would be necessary. This accounts for their very large numbers; allowing a life of five years to each pit and 300 years for the duration of the settlement, Dr. Bersu calculated that the total of approximately 180 pits excavated, with due allowance for the area not examined, meant only three in use at any one time. When they were no longer fit for use as granaries the pits were filled in, partly by the material excavated from their successors and partly by the deposition of rubbish. The seed grain was disposed of differently; since it could not be parched without destroying its fertility, it had to be stored above ground, and hence arose the necessity for the little square granaries raised on posts.

When corn was required for use it was threshed in the hollows referred to above and ground with handmills or querns. The typical quern of Iron Age A, as of the preceding Bronze Age, is the saddle quern, in which the upper stone is rubbed to and fro on the lower. Several fragments of these were found, but before the end of the occupation the rotary quern, initially of a beehive shape, was beginning to come into use.

The investigation of Little Woodbury could not be extended to the fields in which the crops were grown, but surviving traces of field lay-outs elsewhere, which are clearly associated with farms of a similar type and age, leave us in no doubt as to their character. They were the squarish plots, ranging in size from a third to two acres, which, to distinguish them from the strip fields of Saxon and later date, we call 'Celtic' fields (though there is in fact nothing specifically Celtic about them and similar plots occur all over the world at an early stage of agricultural development). Very many groups of them have been identified in this country; some, especially in hilly districts where the field boundaries have formed durable lynchets, are visible on the ground, others can be seen only from the air. Some of the groups are very large, extending to several square miles, and they are sometimes cut through by walled or banked tracks leading to the farmstead. The introduction of this type of field system into Britain goes back at least to the Bronze Age, to which groups in Sussex, Wiltshire and Devon have been dated, but it continued in use and was greatly extended in the Iron Age and Roman period. The shape of the fields suggests that the originators of the system were using the 'ard' rather than the true plough, and the same is probably true of most of their Iron Age successors, but farmers are traditionally conservative and the implications of the continued use of the system in the Roman period will be discussed further below.

But these people did not only grow crops. The Little Woodbury excavations, like most others, produced many bones of ox, sheep, pig, horse and dog, indicating both cattle-rearing and hunting. Cattle do seem in this case to have been of secondary importance to crops, as the farm was sited without reference to a water supply and no trace of a pond was found, nor were there any indications of stalling arrangements, but the balance between agriculture and stock-rearing would vary from region to region. A predominance of the bones of young animals among the household refuse suggests that here, as is the case among some other primitive people, a large proportion of the stock was killed off in the autumn. Other subsidiary activities were pottery-making, a little iron-working, and weaving, which was represented by spindlewhorls of chalk and clay and by a fragment of a bone weaving comb.

The general impression given by Little Woodbury is of a single farmstead, fully large enough to accommodate a family group, but in no sense a village. This is confirmed by less complete excavations elsewhere and it is clear that the single farm, whether constructed in timber, as in Wessex and Sussex, or in stone, as in the West and North, was the normal form of rural habitation throughout the Iron Age. But Little Woodbury belongs culturally to Iron Second A—it was believed by its excavators to have been abandoned by the first century B.C.—and certain reservations must be made in accepting it as typical for the whole period. The most important of these concern its size and its defences. As already noted, the latter were never completed, and they do not occur at all on a number of later sites, notably those excavated by Pitt-Rivers in Cranborne Chase at Rotherley and Woodcuts. Their occurrence here coincides with —one might even say marks the beginning of—that wave of fortification to which we have already referred, and the size of the area enclosed puts it into the same class as the smaller hill forts. Indeed there are a number of sites analogous to it, such as Draughton in Northamptonshire and Queen Mary's Hospital, Carshalton, Surrey, where it is difficult to decide whether the name of farm or hill fort is the more appropriate. Little Woodbury is thus additionally important as exemplifying the transition from the unfortified to the fortified type of settlement.

For the open farms are only one side of the picture. The most notable contribution of the Iron Age to the British landscape was the great fortifications of earth and stone which we know by the name of hill forts or camps. Apart from those in the western coastal region and its extensions, where the type was introduced by B people from Brittany and probably Spain, nearly all the excavated hill forts have revealed an initial phase attributable to Iron Age A, and it is evident that about 250 B.C. southern Britain entered a period of great insecurity. Further, in most excavated examples there have been several periods of construction in their ramparts and gates. With the structural details of these we are not here concerned, but it is possible to draw certain general conclusions from them. The earliest form of hill fort is that of a simple enclosure, very like Little Woodbury, defended by a single rampart and ditch, circular where it is built on level ground but sometimes following the contours of a convenient hill or cutting off a naturally defended promontory. Secondly, still in the cultural phase of A, a number of forts were greatly enlarged in size; the area enclosed at Maiden Castle, Dorset, already unusually great, was increased from fifteen to forty-five acres, and that of many other hill forts, such as Yarnbury and Scratchbury, was more than doubled. Thirdly, usually in the Iron Age B phase, a number of these forts were strengthened by the addition of a second and sometimes a third line of defence. Finally, occupation evidence from the interior proves that many were still in use at the time of the Roman Conquest, and the mass graves belonging to this time, such as those at Maiden Castle and Spettisbury, show that here are some of the twenty *oppida* which Vespasian captured when he commanded the Second Legion.

This account is, of course, oversimplified, and it applies primarily to Wessex, where the evidence is fullest. Even here there are exceptions; it was not only the enlarged forts that were given multiple ramparts and we have examples, such as Spettisbury, of single-ramparted camps still in use at the time of the conquest. Nevertheless, with these reservations, it is possible to discern a tendency for power to become more and more concentrated. For these forts certainly served as centres for the surrounding peasantry and the successive enlargement and strengthening of some, taken together with the absence of such developments in others, must reflect a progressive synoecism of the population. Sometimes, notably in Sussex and in parts of Wessex, it is possible to define the actual area attributable to each fort.

Nor are we entirely without evidence as to the social organization which the hill forts represent. In speaking of the Gauls, with whose customs those of the Britons generally agreed, Caesar observed that only two classes of people were of any account, the Druids and the *Equites*, and he tells how the latter went to war surrounded by large numbers of retainers. He implies that there were a number of *equites* in each tribe, and it is difficult not to see the hill forts as, in effect, their castles, although they differed from mediaeval castles in including demesne land within their fortifications. This interpretation also fits such information as we have regarding their internal arrangements. Though a few of the earliest may have been no more than camps of refuge, the care and labour lavished on their construction in the later period makes it certain that they were then permanently occupied. In the absence of total excavation—an almost impossible task—it is difficult to estimate the density of occupation, but within each tribe it certainly varied greatly from fort to fort, presumably according to how many of his retainers the *eques* wished, or could afford, to keep in permanent attendance. The surrounding peasantry, living in farms that were not normally fortified, would have to bear their part in the work of fortification and would be called in to defend the place in time of trouble. The number of huts noted at Hod Hill and the number implied by the storage pits inside Maiden Castle is considerable, but these, like Ham Hill further to the west, were unusually large and, particularly in view of the peculiar treatment accorded them by the Romans, probably exercised control over other, minor forts, becoming the centres of what the Romans called *pagi*. These are exceptional cases. Taking Wessex as a whole, the nature of the evolution of the forts, their siting, and their numbers all forbid us to see in them any coherent, tribal, strategy. They ended as they began, the individual concern of separate groups or septs within the tribe, not as the defences of the tribe as a whole, and even in their later stages their fortifications must have been directed as much against their immediate neighbours as against any more distant threat. This is not to deny that these people were on occasion capable of acting as a tribe, and a sort of tribal consciousness is proved, at least in some cases, by tribal issues of coins. Whether the Durotriges of Dorset ever recognized a king we do not know, for all their coins are uninscribed; the coins of the Dobunni, centred in Gloucestershire, are inscribed with the names of six dynasts, but the control they exercised over their *equites* can have been no greater than that of the weakest of mediaeval kings over his barons. Seen in this light the multitude of hill forts is no more surprising than the rash of castles which covered mediaeval England.

One of the reasons for this persistent disunity may have been the understandable jealousy for their status of refugee nobles from conquered Gaul and a similar sentiment, in a different context, may account for the erection or refortification of vast numbers of forts in the Welsh Marches when the Romans were conquering southern Britain—many more, indeed, than was strategically sensible. However that may be, it seems to have been general in what we may call the classic hill fort area. This is, roughly speaking, the south and

west of England, with extensions up the Icknield and Jurassic Ways
and along the North and South Downs, and the whole of Wales.

In the eastern part of the country the story is somewhat different.
Here, too, there is an Iron Age A phase—indeed the earliest form of
the culture known in Britain is found at Scarborough and Staple
Howe, in the East Riding of Yorkshire—and here too we have farms
and hill forts. But the latter are much less numerous than in the west
(there are, for example, none at all in Lindsey), and the Iron Age B
invaders of East Yorkshire, Lincolnshire and East Anglia seem to
have had less difficulty in establishing their rule and to have been
more successful in maintaining it thereafter. A corollary of this is
that their cultural influence on their subjects was less pervasive and
our knowledge of them depends much more on their personal
possessions, especially metalwork, and their graves. So far as East
Anglia is concerned, they were early involved either by war or by
trade with their expanding Belgic neighbours.

The Belgae themselves, and especially the people who crossed
over about 100 B.C., formed the most advanced element in the population of Britain. This is stated by Caesar—he refers especially to
Kent—and is reflected both in their farms and in their tribal centres.
Owing to their possession of a superior (though not necessarily
wheeled) type of plough they were able to take advantage of the
more difficult but more rewarding soil of the heavier land, which
their predecessors had left uncleared of its forest. This is a fact of
distribution which was first demonstrated by Sir Cyril Fox in the
Cambridge region, but it applies equally over the whole area of
Belgic settlement. It is partly because of this that we are comparatively ill-informed on the details of Belgic farms, for even when they
have not been mutilated by the superimposition of Roman buildings,
which is often the case, they lie mostly on land which has been
heavily cultivated ever since. Nevertheless we do know that the
single farm was still the normal unit; we know that the usual form of
hut, or huts, was circular; and from the rich burial groups that are
characteristic of the culture we know that in their pottery, which was
normally made on the wheel, and in their metalwork these Belgic
farmers were better, if not always more tastefully, equipped than
their predecessors. In other respects the chief difference from the
Wessex type of farm is that pits are progressively replaced by large

pottery jars for the storage of grain. We also know, from manacles discovered at Park Street and elsewhere, that some Belgic farmers kept slaves.

The difference in their tribal centres is much greater. These were not hill forts, and although there are sites where they took over pre-existing works of this character there are very few cases of their actually having constructed one. In speaking of the headquarters of Cassivellaunus Caesar remarks that 'the Britons call it a town (*oppidum*) when they have fortified dense woodland with a rampart and a ditch'. This description could not be applied to the hill forts of the west, for which upland situations, at most lightly wooded, were chosen, but it suits very well the site at Wheathampstead which has provisionally been identified with the stronghold in question. This is located near a ford over the river Lea on boulder clay, which in its natural condition would be thickly wooded, and despite their immense size the earthworks are not continuous all round it— presumably because the woods made it unnecessary. The area of settlement appears to have been about 100 acres—more than twice that enclosed in the unusually large hill fort of Maiden Castle. But Wheathampstead, as it is the earliest, is also the smallest of the Belgic *oppida* known to us. Both Verulamium and Colchester were considerably larger, though the confusing plan of their dyke defences makes an accurate estimate of their size impossible.

Our knowledge of the internal arrangements of these places is slight. No actual huts were identified on the Belgic site at Verula-mium, though ovens, which had as floors the first 'bricks' to appear in Britain, were discovered; at Colchester what little was found led the excavators to the conclusion that 'the smaller and poorer sort of Belgic dwelling was a structurally primitive and squalid hovel', while a few larger habitations may have been of subrectangular plan. It is not, then, in any splendour of their architecture that the superior civilisation of the Belgae is revealed. Both Verulamium and Col-chester, however, were distinguished by a wealth of foreign pottery imported from the continent, and this requires some further notice.

As we have seen, all the Iron Age peoples of Britain had some Gallic connections, and the existence of these ties was largely respon-sible for the decision of first Caesar and later Claudius to invade the island. In the west, however, although they were strong enough in

56 B.C. for the Veneti of Brittany to send for help from their British cousins, the annihilation of Venetic power by Caesar seems to have led to their relaxation; except on the port site of Hengistbury Head (which also yielded Belgic pottery) later imports from the continent are exceedingly rare. The connections of the Belgae with Gaul were both stronger and more enduring. In the first place, it is evident that they migrated not as individual bands of refugees but as conscious offshoots of tribal units, and Caesar records that in his day many of them retained the names of the Gallic tribes from whom they were sprung; he even states that Diviciacus, the paramount chief of Gaul, included Britain (presumably meaning the Belgic part of it) in his Empire. Secondly, it was they who introduced coinage into Britain, taking as their models the coins of Belgic Gaul. Thirdly, it was because he had great authority in Britain that Caesar sent Commius to Britain. All of this implies a very close community of interest between the people living on either side of the narrow seas.

The imported pottery includes both Mediterranean and Gaulish wares. The latter were the factory-made *terra nigra* and *terra rubra* of central and eastern Gaul, the predecessors of the Gaulish 'Samian', and the former included both fine Arretine from Italy and amphorae, which presumably arrived full of wine and oil. The developing commerce here represented is mentioned by Strabo, who lists the island's chief imports (ivory bracelets and necklaces, amber, glassware and pottery) and exports (corn, cattle, gold, silver, iron, slaves and hunting dogs) and reflects that the loss of the customs duties on them would offset the advantages to be gained by conquest. The effect of this trade, which of course involved merchants as well as merchandise, was that south-east Britain acquired a veneer of romanisation before the Claudian conquest and a familiarity with things Roman which is reflected both in the contents of the Lexden tumulus (not improbably the tomb of Cunobelin himself) and in the style and legends of the later coins of both the chief Belgic kingdoms.

This higher degree of civilisation appears to have been accompanied by greater social stability among the Belgae than among the more primitive peoples who lived to the north and west. But while individualistic hill forts were not tolerated by the Belgic kings, some subdivision of their territory into *pagi* is discernible here too.

Among the Catuvellauni Verulamium was not abandoned when the royal seat was moved to Camulodunum and some minor centres deserve notice, such as Braughing (which has been particularly prolific in coins of both Tasciovanus and Cunobelin) and Dorchester on Thames; while the Atrebatic kingdom had coin mints in two places, at Silchester and Selsey. Moreover if the general run of Belgic *equites* were kept under control, the dynastic quarrels of those of them who claimed royal power made life exciting enough. In Kent, that most civilised district of all, Caesar mentions four men who called themselves kings (*reges*) and after his time the coins indicate that (disregarding the minor dynasts) it fell successively into the hands of Dubnovellaunus, who also ruled over the Trinovantes, of Eppillus, who also ruled the Atrebates, and finally of Cunobelin, of the Catuvellauni. Here the attraction lay in the control of the short sea route to the continent (no doubt the Britons were as ready as the Romans to levy customs duties), but any district on the boundaries of the Catuvellauni was liable to invasion by the army of Cunobelin, whose very success implies a higher degree of organisation. The spread of Belgic influence, however, was not confined to those areas, large as they were, which Cunobelin incorporated in his empire. Belgic ideas reflected in pottery types and in the use of coinage—the latter probably implying in most cases the imposition of a Belgic dynasty—can be traced as far west as Camerton in Somerset and Bagendon in Gloucestershire, as far north as Loughborough in Leicestershire and Scunthorpe in Lincolnshire, and over much of East Anglia. The latest pottery in these areas of secondary Belgic influence is made on the wheel and usually combines local traditions with Belgic forms, while the coins are in each case derived from the same models as the early Catuvellaunian (formerly called 'Atrebatic') or Atrebatic (formerly called 'Remic') issues. In view of this development it is possible to group the peoples of Britain at the time of the Roman conquest into three classes: first, the Belgic tribes themselves, second, the tribes displaying the secondary Belgic characteristics just referred to, and third, the tribes of the hinterland who were still immune to Belgic influence.

In the first class are the Catuvellauni, the Atrebates and probably the Trinovantes. The main centres of the Catuvellauni were at Camulodunum and Verulamium and their empire, as indicated by the distribution of coins of Cunobelin, included not only the modern counties of Hertfordshire and Essex, but also Northamptonshire, Huntingdonshire, Cambridgeshire, Bedfordshire, Buckinghamshire, Middlesex, the eastern half of Oxfordshire, north-east Surrey and most of Kent; in addition, Cunobelin seems to have gained control of the northern part of the Atrebatic kingdom, from north Wiltshire and Berkshire to west Surrey. The Atrebatic kingdom itself was centred on Silchester and Selsey and included Berkshire, north-east Wiltshire, Hampshire, west Surrey and west Sussex. The right of the Trinovantes to be included in the first category is not established and they are frequently referred to as a non-Belgic tribe. There is certainly a substratum of Iron Age A culture in their area, as there is in most of south-east Britain, but there is little trace of B, and there are three definite pointers to their character. First, and most important, Caesar describes them as 'about the strongest tribe in those parts' in his day, which accords ill with our knowledge not only of Iron Age A cultures in general but of that of this district in particular; secondly, the distribution of Belgic pedestal urns strongly suggests a spread up the rivers from the coast as well as a spread eastwards from the Catuvellauni; and thirdly, the coins of the Trinovantes, especially those of Addedomaros and Dubnovellaunus, are fully as sophisticated as those of their Catuvellaunian neighbours. The Trinovantian centre was Camulodunum and they occupied much of Essex and Suffolk, but both their capital and the southern part of their territory were conquered by the Catuvellauni and their boundaries and their history in the immediate pre-conquest period are alike obscure.

The second class includes the Iceni, the Coritani, the Dobunni and the Durotriges. Among the Iceni there is again a substratum of Iron Age A, but Iron Age B is also represented by chariot burials and there was probably a phase of domination by immigrant chieftains before the C influences appear. The distribution of Icenian coins suggests the existence of two centres, one near Norwich and one in the Breckland, and their territory included the whole of Norfolk and the north-west part of Suffolk. The Coritani inhabited Leicestershire, Rutland, Lincolnshire, Nottinghamshire, and possibly a little of south Yorkshire. Here too there is an A basis with a B influence, including chariot burials, but the final pre-Roman phase is characterised by the appearance of Belgic-type pottery not only in those parts which were already settled but in other districts as well. The recent convincing demonstration by Mr. D. F. Allen that the coins formerly attributed to the Brigantes belong, together with some uninscribed types, to the Coritani, lends point to this distribution and suggests that here too we have a Belgic dynasty imposing itself upon a non-Belgic people. One centre was at Leicester, where traces of a Belgic settlement have been found beneath the Roman town, while the discovery of a coin mint suggests the existence of another at Old Sleaford.

The coinage of both the Iceni and the Coritani is related to the Catuvellaunian issues. That of the Dobunni, on the other hand, derives from the 'Remic' stem and has close affinities with the coins of the Atrébates. The Dobunni occupied Gloucestershire and extended south into Somerset and north Wiltshire, east as far as the Cherwell, west into Herefordshire and north into Worcestershire and Warwickshire. The A element in their make-up is most noticeable in the southern and eastern part of their territory, and even there it is overlaid by B, and their strongest connections were with the B peoples of the south-west. Hill forts are numerous both in the Cotswolds and in Herefordshire, much fewer in the north-east. Belgic influences appear late, possibly no more than a generation before the Roman conquest, and are seen first in the adoption of a coinage, second in C pottery forms and technique on a few of the sites already occupied, such as Salmonsbury, and thirdly in the appearance of at least two large settlements defended by dykes in the Belgic fashion, at Minchinhampton and Bagendon. Excavation of a small part of the latter has revealed the existence of a coin mint, and in view of this, coupled with its proximity to Cirencester, where the Romans established the tribal capital, there is little doubt that it was the royal seat in the period immediately before the conquest. The relations between this Belgic, or Belgicising, dynasty and the Iron Age B barons already established in the country is not yet clear, but it may be significant that in the northern half of the Dobunnic territory their coins have not yet been found in hill forts, except at Salmonsbury, but are widely if thinly distributed in the heavier land of Worcestershire.

The last of the coin-using tribes, the Durotriges, occupied Dorset,

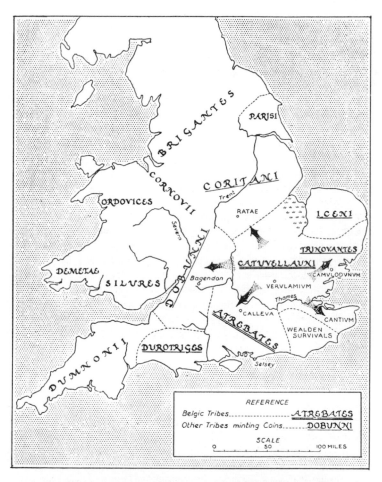

FIG. 1. Britain at the time of the Roman conquest, showing approximate tribal areas and main lines of Catuvellaunian expansion

south Wiltshire, south Somerset, and east Devon. They were the dominant tribe of Wessex and their earlier development has already been dealt with above, but interpretation of their final phase is peculiarly difficult. While they adopted coinage comparatively early, in their hands it degenerated rather than developed, first abandoning gold for silver only, then silver for bronze, and ended up with some most barbarous coins which were not struck but cast, and alone of all the coin-using tribes they never produced inscribed issues. Their latest pre-Roman pottery was made on the wheel, but its most common forms remained those which were in vogue in the B phase and the amount of Belgic influence here is controversial. Finally, they remained, in contrast to the Belgae, essentially a hill fort people. The probable explanation of all these phenomena is, in broad terms, that Wessex was the refuge of all those recalcitrant elements, whether in Gaul under Caesar and Augustus or in Britain under Cunobelin, who valued their independence above their comforts. There is no one recognisable capital of the Durotriges. The Roman capital was established at Dorchester, which has been taken to point to Maiden Castle, but there was a mint at Hengistbury Head, and Hod Hill, Ham Hill and Badbury Rings could all, for varying reasons, lay claim to something like equality. The picture seems to be that of a loose federation rather than a monolithic nation, and if the disadvantages of this state of affairs are shown in the comparative poverty of the people, it had its advantages too; Wessex was not conquered until Vespasian had stormed twenty different fortresses.

With two exceptions the tribes in the third category lay to the north and west of the areas we have so far discussed. The exceptions cannot be named with certainty, though one is no doubt included among the tribes mentioned by Caesar and we know what the Romans later called the other. The former occupied an area of east Sussex, east Surrey and south-west Kent. They were the heirs of the culture known as 'South-Eastern Second B' and appear to have maintained their Wealden enclave against Belgic penetrations from east and west alike. Their centres were hill forts of which the best known, though by no means the largest, is the Caburn, near Lewes. The second group of people were those who occupied central Wiltshire, including Salisbury Plain, westwards towards Bath. This

area shared in the earlier development of Wessex, but in the later
phase it is peculiarly unproductive of coins and does not appear to
have been affiliated to either the Durotriges or the Dobunni. It was
included by the Romans in the canton of the Belgae, whose capital
was Winchester, and Belgic pottery is common, but evidence is
lacking of a fully organised Belgic state.

Of the peripheral tribes the largest was the Brigantes. In Roman
times they are described by Ptolemy as occupying the whole of
England north of the Coritani and the Cornovii, except for the East
Riding of Yorkshire. Compared with the southern tribes they were
a backward people and so far as it is known their economy was still
largely that of the Bronze Age, Iron Age influences being represented by a few hill forts and chariot burials; the latter are clearly
related to those of the Parisi of the East Riding. Brigantia is divided
by nature into a number of well-defined areas and this fact seems to
have been reflected politically in a loose confederation of peoples,
under a paramount king or, as in early Roman times, queen. Apart
from the few hill forts of normal size and form, excavation has
shown that the phenomenal earthworks at Stanwick, eight miles
north of Richmond, which in their final phase enclosed an area of
730 acres, were their work and probably the scene of their final
stand against the Romans.

The Parisi of the East Riding conform more nearly to the
southern pattern of development. An early population of Iron Age
A connections was there subjected to the rule of B invaders whose
country of origin, as evidenced both by their name and by their
remains, especially their chariot burials, was the Seine-Marne region
of France. The most notable occupation site so far investigated is
at Elmswell near Driffield, but the political organisation of the tribe
is unknown. The Roman name of Brough-on-Humber, Petuaria
(the P-Celtic equivalent of the Latin *Quarta*), may indicate that they
were grouped in four *pagi*.

The Cornovii were centred in Shropshire and extended northwards into Cheshire, eastwards into Staffordshire and westwards
into Denbigh and Montgomery. The basic population probably
remained the old Bronze Age stock, but hill forts of Iron Age type
are numerous. Pottery comparable with that of the First A phase in
Wessex was used in the earliest occupation of Old Oswestry and the

few sherds recovered in excavations on the Wrekin were generally of Iron Age A character, but insufficient evidence is available to see clearly the connections of the people, and methods of fortification often transgress cultural boundaries. There is as yet no evidence of any central organisation and the Cornovii may have been, like the Brigantes, a loose confederation rather than a tribe in the full sense of the word.

Much the same may also be true of the Silures, who dwelt in Monmouth and Glamorgan, though their affinities are a little clearer. The first-century cliff castles of Gower are similar to those of Cornwall and another link with the south-west is discernible in the abnormal siting of the 'hill-slope forts' which occur in both regions. In the eastern part of their territory, as at Llanmelin Wood, near Caerwent, pottery analogous to that of some of the Dobunnic hill forts occurs, together with some suggesting Belgic influence. Of the Demetae, of Pembrokeshire and Carmarthenshire, little can be said beyond the fact that their earthworks are again most closely paralleled in Cornwall. The rest of Wales, whose inhabitants included the Ordovices and the Deceangli, never seems to have emerged from direct rule in the Roman period and so falls outside the scope of this book.

The last of the peripheral tribes is in some ways the most interesting. The Dumnonii occupied the whole south-western peninsula west of the river Exe. Both on Dartmoor and in Penwith the transition from the Bronze Age to the Iron Age seems to follow a local course, with little foreign intervention, beyond what is implied by the introduction of the new metallurgy. Around the coasts, however, and in the lower country generally, foreign influences are clear, especially in Cornwall. West of the Tamar very few earthworks bear any resemblance to the normal hill fort types of Wessex. The majority are either cliff castles, identical with those of southern Brittany, or ringworks, frequently with a wide space between their inner and outer defences—a type which seems to have originated in Spain and which spreads eastwards into Devonshire. These Dumnonii are the people called hospitable by Pytheas —the actual word in Diodorus Siculus is φιλόξενοι, 'friendly to strangers'—and besides St. Michael's Mount, which has been identified with their emporium of Ictis, miscellaneous finds indicate the existence of a trading port at Mount Batten; but no tribal centre has been identified and the Roman choice of Exeter seems to have been dictated by other than local considerations.

In summary, then, the Britain which confronted the Romans was occupied by a number of Celtic tribes whose composition, social structure and degree of economic development varied considerably. The most advanced were the people of the south-east, where a stable central government had been established over a wide area and where settlement was no longer confined to the easier lands. Militarily, their civilisation was both their strength and their weakness; for although Caratacus and Togodumnus could raise a better organised and better armed force than any other leaders in Britain, when once their army was beaten the war was over, and the minor states subjected to the Catuvellauni would gladly come to terms with Rome. The more protracted fighting was against the tribes of the hinterland, to whom freedom was more than a word and whose natural situation and social organisation alike fitted them for guerilla warfare. Nevertheless the influence of the Belgae extended, directly or indirectly, to many of these tribes too. It was probably because of the existence of Belgic ruling families among them that Caratacus could move so freely from tribe to tribe in his long struggle with Rome, and the fact that Cartimandua of the Brigantes betrayed him does not disprove a relationship. In the economic sphere the evidence is growing that wherever the Belgae went there was a tendency for the heavier land to be brought under cultivation and the primitive pattern of settlement to be modified. And the close agreement of the area involved with that of the civilised part of Roman Britain strongly suggests that it was these people, rude and uncultured though they were, who laid the foundations on which the prosperity of the Roman province ultimately rested.

BIBLIOGRAPHY

A work of fundamental importance for the understanding of any part of British prehistory is C. Fox: *The Personality of Britain* (National Museum of Wales, 4th edn., 1944), and the same writer's *The Archaeology of the Cambridge Region* (C.U.P., 1923, reprinted 1948) has a more than local significance.

There is as yet no major work devoted to the British Iron Age. Good general accounts are included in C. & J. Hawkes: *Prehistoric Britain* (Penguin, 1958) and in V. G. Childe: *Prehistoric Communities of the British Isles* (Chambers, 3rd edn., 1949). The grouping of Iron Age cultures as A, B and C was first propounded in C. F. C. Hawkes' article 'Hill Forts', in *Antiquity*, v, 1931, and elaborated in Kendrick & Hawkes: *Archaeology in England and Wales, 1914–1931* (Methuen, 1932, out of print); and the latter is, from a technical point of view, the best starting point. More recent summaries are the Iron Age section of *A Survey and Policy of Field Research in the Archaeology of Great Britain*, I (Council for British Archaeology, 1948) and C. A. R. Radford: 'The Tribes of Southern Britain' (*Procs. Prehistoric Soc.*, XVIII, 1955). (See also p. 59.)

For Iron Age A, K. M. Kenyon: 'A Survey of the Evidence concerning the Chronology and Origins of Iron Age A in Southern and Midland Britain' (University of London Institute of Archaeology, *Eighth Annual Report*, 1952) is a useful review of the pottery with an excellent bibliography. For Iron Age C the fundamental work is C. F. C. Hawkes and G. C. Dunning: 'The Belgae of Gaul and Britain' (*Archaeological Journal*, LXXXVII, 1930).

For regional surveys, the volumes of the Victoria County Histories are not as a rule helpful, because most of the prehistoric articles were written before the subject had developed; exceptions are *Cambridgeshire* (by J. G. D. Clark, I, 1938), *Huntingdonshire* (by C. Fox, M. C. Burkitt & G. Wyman Abbott, I, 1926), *Oxfordshire* (by H. N. Savory, I, 1939) and *Wiltshire* (gazetteer by L. V. Grinsell, I (i), 1957, discussion by C. F. C. Hawkes, I (ii), forthcoming). To these may be added the volumes in the County Archaeologies Series referred to in Chapter 1 (especially *Sussex*) and a number of papers in national and county journals, notably the following:

L. Alcock: 'Celtic Archaeology and Art' (in *Celtic Studies in Wales*, University of Wales, 1963).

J. W. Brailsford: 'Iron Age C in Wessex' (*Procs. Prehistoric Soc.*, forthcoming).

R. R. Clarke: 'The Iron Age in Norfolk and Suffolk' (*Archaeological Journal*, XCVI, 1939).

M. A. Cotton: 'Berkshire Hill Forts' (*Berks. Archaeol. Journal* LX, 1962).

A. Fox: 'Hill-Slope Forts and Related Earthworks in South-West England and South Wales' (*Archaeological Journal*, CIX, 1952).

S. S. Frere: 'An Iron Age Site at West Clandon, Surrey, and Some Aspects of Iron Age and Romano-British Culture in the Wealden Area' (*Archaeological Journal*, CI, 1944).

C. F. C. Hawkes: 'Hampshire and the British Iron Age, 1905–1955' (*Procs. Hants Field Club and Archaeological Soc.*, XX, 1956).

C. F. C. Hawkes and S. Piggott: 'Britons, Romans and Saxons round Salisbury and in Cranborne Chase' (*Archaeological Journal*, CIV, 1947).

W. J. Varley: 'The Hill-Forts of the Welsh Marches' (*Archaeological Journal*, CV, 1948).

A. E. Wilson and G. P. Burstow: 'The Evolution of Sussex Iron Age Pottery' (*Sussex Archaeological Collections*, LXXXVII, 1948).

A. E. Wilson: 'Sussex on the Eve of the Roman Conquest' (*Sussex Archaeological Collections*, XCIII, 1955).

Regional surveys are also appended to many of the reports on individual sites, and for this reason the following list, while primarily supplying references for sites mentioned in the text, includes also a few additions:

Hill Forts

Badbury Rings, Dorset: O. G. S. Crawford and A. Keiller: *Wessex from the Air* (O.U.P., 1928).

Bredon Hill, Glos: T. C. Hencken in *Archaeological Journal*, XCV, 1938.

Breedon Hill, Leics: K. M. Kenyon in *Trans. Leics Archaeological Soc.*, XXVI, 1950.

Bury Walls, Hants: C. F. C. Hawkes in *Procs. Hants Fd. Club and Archaeological Soc.*, XIV, 1940.

The Caburn, Sussex: A. E. Wilson in *Sussex Archaeological Collns.*, LXXIX, 1938 and LXXX, 1939 (with review of pottery by C. F. C. Hawkes in the latter).

Chun Castle, Cornwall: E. T. Leeds in *Archaeologia*, LXXXI, 1931.

Ffridd Faldwyn, Montgomery: B. St. J. O'Neil in *Archaeologia Cambrensis*, XCVII, 1943.

Gower Peninsula, Glamorgan: A. Williams in *Archaeologia Cambrensis*, XCIV, 1939, XCV, 1940, and XCVI, 1941.

Gurnard's Head, Cornwall: A. S. R. Gordon in *Archaeological Journal*, XCVII, 1940.

Ham Hill, Somerset: H. St. G. Gray in *Procs. Somerset Archaeological and Nat. Hist. Soc.*, LXX, 1924, LXXI, 1925, and LXXII, 1926.

Hembury, Devon: D. Liddell in *Procs. Devon Archaeological Exploration Soc.*, I, 1929–32.

Hengistbury Head, Hants: J. P. Bushe-Fox: 'Hengistbury Head' (*Soc. of Antiquaries Research Report III*, 1915).

Hod Hill, Dorset: O. G. S. Crawford and A. Keiller: *Wessex from the Air* (O.U.P., 1928) and brief reports on recent excavations by I. A. Richmond and J. W. Brailsford in *Journal of Roman Studies*, XLII, 1952, onwards.

Hunsbury, Northants: C. I. Fell in *Archaeological Journal*, XCIII, 1936.

Llanmelin, Monmouth: V. E. Nash-Williams in *Archaeologia Cambrensis*, LXXXVIII, 1933.

Lydney, Glos: R. E. M. and T. V. Wheeler: 'Lydney Park' (*Soc. of Antiquaries Research Report IX*, 1932).

Maiden Castle, Dorset: R. E. M. Wheeler: 'Maiden Castle' (*Soc. of Antiquaries Research Report XII*, 1943).

Oldbury, Kent: J. B. Ward Perkins in *Archaeologia*, XC, 1944.

Old Oswestry, Salop: W. J. Varley in *Archaeological Journal*, CV, 1948, and unpublished.

St. Catharine's Hill, Hants: C. F. C. Hawkes, J. N. L. Myres and C. G. Stevens: 'St. Catharine's Hill' (*Procs. Hants Fd. Club and Archaeological Soc.*, XI, 1930).

St. Mawgan-in-Pyder, Cornwall: L. Murray Threipland in *Archaeological Journal*, CXIII, 1956.

Salmonsbury, Glos: G. C. Dunning in *Antiquity*, V, 1931.

Scratchbury, Wilts: O. G. S. Crawford and A. Keiller: *Wessex from the Air* (O.U.P., 1928); recent excavations (unpublished) have shown the inner defences to be of Iron Age, not Neolithic, date.

Spettisbury Rings, Dorset: C. A. Gresham in *Archaeological Journal*, XCVI, 1939.

Sutton Walls, Hereford: K. M. Kenyon in *Archaeological Journal*, CX, 1953.

The Trundle, Sussex: E. C. Curwen in *Sussex Archaeological Collns.*, LXX, 1929.

The Wrekin, Salop: K. M. Kenyon in *Archaeological Journal*, XCIX, 1942.

Yarnbury, Wilts: M. E. Cunnington in *Wilts Archaeological Mag.*, XLVI, 1932–4.

For comparative material in Gaul see R. E. M. Wheeler and K. M. Richardson: 'Hill Forts of Northern France' (*Soc. of Antiquaries Research Report*, XIX, 1957).

Other Sites

All Cannings Cross, Wilts: M. E. Cunnington: *All Cannings Cross* (privately, Devizes, 1923).

Bagendon, Glos.: E. M. Clifford: *Bagendon, a Belgic Oppidum* (Heffer, 1961).

Braughing, Herts: M. V. Taylor in *V.C.H. Herts*, IV, 1914, and J. Holmes in *Trans. E. Herts Archaeological Soc.*, XIII, 1953.

Camerton, Somerset: W. J. Wedlake: *The Excavations at Camerton, Somerset*, 1958.

Camulodunum (Colchester), Essex: C. F. C. Hawkes and M. R. Hull: 'Camulodunum' (*Soc. of Antiquaries Research Report*, XIV, 1947).

Crayford, Kent: J. B. Ward Perkins in *Procs. Prehistoric Soc.*, IV, 1938.

Dartmoor, Devon: C. A. R. Radford in *Procs. Prehistoric Soc.*, XVIII, 1952, and A. Fox in *Procs. Prehistoric Soc.*, XX, 1955.

Dorchester, Oxon: H. N. Savory in *V.C.H. Oxon*, I, 1939.

Dorchester (Allen's Pit), Oxon: J. S. P. Bradford in *Oxoniensia*, VII, 1942.

Draughton, Northants: Excavated by W. F. Grimes, report forthcoming.

Elmswell, E.R. Yorks: A. L. Congreve: *Elmswell I & II* (Hull Museum Pubns. 193 & 198, 1936–7) and P. Corder: *Elmswell III* (Hull University, 1940).

Fengate (Peterborough), Northants: C. F. C. Hawkes in *Archaeological Journal*, C, 1943.

Frilford, Berks: J. S. P. Bradford and R. G. Goodchild in *Oxoniensia*, IV, 1939.

Glastonbury, Somerset: A. Bulleid and H. St. G. Gray: 'The Glastonbury Lake Village' (2 vols., *Glastonbury Antiquarian Soc.*, 1911 and 1917).

Leicester: K. M. Kenyon: 'The Jewry Wall Site, Leicester' (*Soc. of Antiquaries Research Report*, XV, 1948).

Lexden Tumulus, Essex: P. Laver in *Archaeologia*, LXXVI, 1927.

Loughborough, Leics: K. M. Kenyon in *Trans. Leics Archaeological Soc.*, XXVI, 1950 (p. 52).

Meare, Somerset: A. Bulleid and H. St. G. Gray: *The Meare Lake Village* (2 vols., privately, Taunton, 1948 and 1953) and H. St. G. Gray in *Procs. Somerset Arch. and Nat. Hist. Soc.* up to CI and CII, 1958.

Minchinhampton, Glos: E. M. Clifford in *Trans. Bristol and Glos Archaeological Soc.*, LIX, 1937.

Mount Batten, Devon: C. S. Bate in *Archaeologia*, XL, 1866.

Old Sleaford: Mrs. M. T. Jones in *Journal of Roman Studies*, LI, 1961, p. 171, and LII, 1962, p. 167.

Park Brow, Sussex: G. R. Wolseley, R. A. Smith and W. Hawley in *Archaeologia*, LXXVI, 1927.

Park Street, Herts: H. E. O'Neil in *Archaeological Journal*, CII, 1945.

Penwith, Cornwall: H. O'N. Hencken: 'Excavns. at Chysauster' in *Archaeologia*, LXXXIII, 1933; H. O'N. Hencken: *Cornwall and Scilly* (County Archaeologies, Methuen, 1932); F. C. Hirst: 'Excavns. at Porthmeor' in *Journal of the Royal Institution of Cornwall*, XXIV, 1937 (App. II); D. Dudley: 'Excavn. at Bodrifty' in *Archaeological Journal*, CXIII, 1956.

Queen Mary's Hospital, Carshalton, Surrey: A. W. G. Lowther in *Surrey Archaeological Collns.*, XLIX, 1946.

Rotherley, Wilts: C. F. C. Hawkes and S. Piggott in 'Britons, Romans and Saxons' (*Archaeological Journal*, CIV, 1947).

Runcton Holme, Norfolk: C. F. C. Hawkes in *Procs. Prehistoric Soc. of East Anglia*, VII, 1933.

Scarborough, E.R. Yorks: R. E. M. Wheeler in Rowntree (ed.): *History of Scarborough* (Dent, 1931).

Scunthorpe, Lincs: H. Dudley: *Early Days in N.W. Lincolnshire* (Caldicott, Scunthorpe, 1949).

Selsey, Sussex: E. C. Curwen: *Sussex* (County Archaeologies, Methuen, 2nd edn., 1954).

Silchester, Hants: G. C. Boon: *Roman Silchester* (Parrish, 1957).

Standlake, Oxon: J. S. P. Bradford in *Antiquaries Journal*, XXII, 1942.

Stanwick, N.R. Yorks: R. E. M. Wheeler: 'The Stanwick Fortifications' (*Soc. of Antiquaries Research Report*, XVII, 1954).

Staple Howe, E.R. Yorks: T. C. M. Brewster: *The Excavation of Staple Howe* (E. Riding Archaeological Society, 1963).

Stone, Kent: M. A. Cotton and K. M. Richardson in *Procs. Prehistoric Soc.*, VII, 1941.

Verulamium (St. Albans), Herts: R. E. M. and T. V. Wheeler: 'Verulamium' (*Soc. of Antiquaries Research Report*, XI, 1936).

West Harling, Norfolk: H. Apling in *Procs. Prehistoric Soc. of East Anglia*, VII, 1932, and J. G. D. Clark and C. I. Fell in *Procs. Prehistoric Soc.*, XIX, 1953.

Wheathampstead, Herts: R. E. M. and T. V. Wheeler: 'Verulamium' (*Soc. of Antiquaries Research Report*, XI, 1936).

Woodbury, Wilts: G. Bersu in *Procs. Prehistoric Soc.*, VI, 1940, and J. W. Brailsford in *Procs. Prehistoric Soc.*, XIV, 1948, and XV, 1949.

Woodcuts, Dorset: C. F. C. Hawkes and S. Piggott in 'Britons, Romans and Saxons' (*Archaeological Journal*, CIV, 1947).

Communications

The course of the Icknield Way is shown on the quarter-inch and one-inch Ordnance Survey maps, and on the *Map of Roman Britain*. The same is true of the Harroway and the North Downs Trackway; on the latter, see also I. D. Margary: 'The North Downs Trackway and The Pilgrims' Way' in *Archaeological Journal*, CIX, 1952. On the Jurassic Way, see W. F. Grimes in *Aspects of Archaeology* (Edwards, 1951).

Currency

On the iron currency bars in use in Wessex and the Cotswolds before the introduction of coinage, see C. Fox in *Antiquity*, XIV, 1940.

On coins the standard work is J. Evans: *The Coins of the Ancient Britons* (1864, supplement 1890). More recent is R. P. Mack: *The Coinage of Ancient Britain* (Spink, 1953), which includes a number of types identified since Evans but also omits a few. Other important works on this subject are:

G. C. Brooke: 'The Philippus in the West and the Belgic Invasions of Britain' (*Numismatic Chronicle*, 5th series, XIII, 1933).

G. C. Brooke: 'The Distribution of Gaulish and British Coins in Britain' (*Antiquity*, VII, 1933).

D. F. Allen: 'The Belgic Dynasties of Britain and their Coins' (*Archaeologia*, XC, 1944); this is particularly valuable for the chronology of the later period.

R. H. M. Dolley: Note on the Speculum Coinage of Britain appended to R. R. Clarke: 'The Early Iron Age Treasure from Snettisham, Norfolk' (*Procs. Prehistoric Soc.*, XX, 1954).

For the attribution of the 'Brigantian' coinage to the Coritani see D. F. Allen: *The Coins of the Coritani* (British Academy, 1963).

On the Greek and other Mediterranean coins imported into Britain, possibly in the Iron Age, see J. G. Milne: *Finds of Greek Coins in the British Isles* (O.U.P., 1948).

Religion and Art

On Druidism, see T. D. Kendrick: *The Druids* (Methuen, 2nd edn., 1928).

On Celtic gods in general, see chapter V of I. A. Richmond: *Roman Britain* (Penguin, 1963) and the bibliography appended thereto.

On Celtic Art, see C. Fox: *Pattern and Purpose* (National Museum of Wales, 1958).

Political Relations with Rome

See especially C. E. Stevens: 'Britain between the Invasions (54 B.C.–A.D. 43)' in Grimes (ed.) : *Aspects of Archaeology* (Edwards, 1951).

Additional Bibliography

S. S. Frere (ed.): *Problems of the Iron Age in Southern Britain* (University of London Institute of Archaeology Occasional Paper No. 11, 1961). This is the report of the C.B.A. conference held in December, 1958, and among other important papers includes C. F. C. Hawkes: 'The A.B.C. of the British Iron Age', setting out his revised cultural and chronological scheme, and D. F. Allen: 'The Origins of Coinage in Britain', with a revised classification of the coins and a complete gazetteer of their find-spots.

The Ordnance Survey Map of Southern Britain in the Iron Age, 1962. The booklet accompanying the map includes a general introduction to the period (by the present author) and an important study (by D. F. Allen) of the tribal coinages, illustrated by eight distribution maps, besides an index to the sites shown on the main map.

T. G. E. Powell: *The Celts* (Thames and Hudson, 1958). This surveys the evidence for the origins and history of the Celts in their wider international setting.

3

ROMAN ADMINISTRATION

Singulos sibi olim reges fuisse, nunc binos imponi, e quibus
legatus in sanguinem, procurator in bona saeviret.

> TACITUS (late first century) on the British
> reaction to Roman rule.

Dumque offers victis proprii consortia iuris
Urbem fecisti quod prius orbis erat.

> RUTILIUS NAMATIANUS (early fifth century)
> on the achievement of Rome.

Cassius Dio tells us that when the forces for the Claudian invasion of Britain were assembled on the shores of Gaul, the soldiers mutinied on the grounds that they were being asked to serve ἔξω τῆς οἰκουμένης. The phrase is difficult to translate: literally, as it is used by the geographers, it means 'outside the inhabited world', but it is sometimes employed loosely to mean 'outside the civilised (i.e. Greek or Roman) world'. In any case, the incident is so vivid and memorable that it can easily lead one into the belief that the conquest of Britain did in fact represent a venture into the unknown. That this was not so, however it may have appeared to the common soldiery, is shown by the evidence of archaeology and literature alike. In addition to the commercial developments mentioned in the last chapter, Rome already had some political ties with Britain.

When Julius Caesar left the island after his second expedition, he had concluded treaties with some of the tribes and laid down the amount of tribute they should pay. In effect the rulers of these tribes had become client kings of Rome—an arrangement which was commonly adopted on the fringes of the Roman world. For how long, if at all, the tribute was paid is uncertain, and some of Caesar's political instructions were certainly disregarded. For instance, he had forbidden the Catuvellauni to attack the Trinovantes, yet a generation later they not only attacked them but conquered them and set up their new capital at Camulodunum, in Trinovantian territory. Two British princes, Dubnovellaunus and Tincommius, sought refuge with Augustus, and according to Cassius Dio he twice planned an invasion, in 34 and again in 27 B.C., but on each occasion he was prevented by having more urgent matters to attend to elsewhere. The emperor Gaius, in A.D. 40, actually assembled an army for this purpose, again after the flight to him of a British prince, Amminius. And finally it was the complaint of yet another exile, Bericus or Verica, which gave Claudius his *casus belli*. These facts are known to us, as it were, by chance, and there is little doubt that the full diplomatic dossier would reveal a more or less continuous Roman concern in British affairs. It would not have been impossible for the Roman delegate to some unimaginable United Nations to present the Claudian invasion, if not as a purely internal matter, at least as a campaign of pacification in a legitimate sphere of Roman interest.

In view of this it is not surprising that in some cases the Britons were, to begin with, treated not as subjects in the full sense but rather as client kingdoms with which Claudius established treaty relationships. We know of three kingdoms which were dealt with in this way: the Iceni in Norfolk, the Brigantes in Yorkshire, and the kingdom of Cogidubnus, which was centred on Chichester. There may well have been more—the Dobunni are a possibility—but in any case they were short-lived. Cogidubnus, so Tacitus says, remained reliable up to his own time, but there is no indication that any son succeeded him; the Iceni were forcibly incorporated as soon as Prasutagus died; and the constant intrigues of Venutius and Cartimandua gave Rome ample excuse for bringing the Brigantian dynasty to an end. After the first century kings have no place in Roman Britain and we may disregard them in considering the political organisation of the provinces.

The system of Roman provincial government in force at the time Britain was conquered was that introduced by Augustus. According to the old republican tradition, provinces had been governed by men who had just held important magistracies in Rome itself, either by proconsuls or by propraetors. Originally such governors had held office for one year only, but when, with the extension of Roman rule, the number of provinces outran the number of suitable magistrates, an amendment had been introduced whereby their tenure could be extended by the senate. Even in this modified form such an arrangement was obviously unsatisfactory. For one thing no one knew in advance if he would have more than one year as governor—and whether or not he did so depended on a number of things, some of them involving corrupt practices. But even more important was the fact that the governor was also the commander-in-chief, and not everyone who made a good consul or praetor made a good general. This had been met to some extent by the conferring of extraordinary commands on men like Pompey, but that did not improve the basic situation. When Augustus established himself after the civil wars, he could not simply take upon himself the appointment of governors, for that would have run counter to his propaganda theme of 'restoring the Republic'. Instead, he so arranged it that he himself was granted the oversight of all those territories where large bodies of troops were stationed (and some others) as his province; the term had never necessarily implied a compact piece of land. His province thus consisted of rather more than half the empire and for convenience he governed it through legates. Since these officers had sometimes been used by provincial governors in the good old days of the Republic, here too he still conformed to republican practice. After its conquest Britain was included among these so-called imperial provinces and so in law the governor was the Emperor himself, but for practical purposes it was a man appointed by him, a *legatus Augusti pro praetore*.

In Britain, as in other important military commands, the *legatus* was a man of senatorial rank and carefully selected for his task. Under him, as Commander-in-Chief, were the *legati legionum* (the commanders of the individual legions) and the *praefecti* of the units of auxiliaries, and he was also responsible for the civil government of the province, including the administration of justice. In this sphere, however, when the military burden was very heavy, an additional officer was sometimes appointed to assist him. In Britain we know the names of five such *legati iuridici* and two of them, Javolenus Priscus and Salvius Liberalis, were lawyers of very great distinction. They both held office in the last fifteen years of the first century, and while their appointments must have been made to relieve the governor for military duties in the north it is possible that their special task was concerned with the reconciliation of Celtic and Roman Law. It has even been suggested that this was the sort of legateship held by Cogidubnus.

But there was one field over which the power of the *legatus* did not extend. A separate officer, the *procurator Augusti*, was directly responsible to the Emperor for finance, including the collection of taxes. It was a procurator, Decianus Catus, whose rapacity was largely to blame for the Boudiccan revolt, and it was another, Julius Classicianus, whose direct approach to Nero secured the replacement of the *legatus*, Suetonius Paulinus, when his repression of the revolt became too savage.

These men, with their staffs, were responsible for the central government of the province. But Roman provincial government was not entirely centralised. Some areas, it is true, remained subject to military rule, and others, the Emperor's private estates, were administered directly for him by procurators, but in the civilised part of the province there was a great deal of local autonomy. In the first place, four towns held the rank of *Colonia*, that is to say they were towns of Roman citizens. Three of them were settlements of veterans from legions, planted as an act of deliberate policy, an application of the common Roman principle of giving pensions in land rather than in money and at the same time creating a reliable reserve in time of emergency. The first was Camulodunum, founded at Colchester in A.D. 49, probably for veterans of the 14th and 20th legions. The second, Lindum Colonia, was founded at Lincoln about 92 for veterans of the 9th legion; and the third, Colonia Nervia Glevensis, was founded at Gloucester in 97 for veterans of the 2nd legion. The last *colonia*, that at York (Eburacum), whose foundation date we do not know, seems to represent a grant of the status to a settlement which had grown up spontaneously beside the fortress of the 6th legion.

These *coloniae* enjoyed local government and their constitutions were modelled on that of Rome itself. As at Rome, their magistrates were appointed in pairs and held office for one year. The senior pair were the *duoviri iure dicundo*, who were responsible especially for the adminstration of justice; the second pair were the *duoviri aediles*, who had the oversight of roads, buildings and public order; and in some *coloniae* (though we have no evidence for this in Britain) there were also two quaestors, who dealt with finance. In theory all these officers should have been elected by the *comitia* or popular assembly, but, as at Rome itself, this practice died out and from the second century at least magistrates nominated their successors, subject to the approval of the *decuriones*. These decurions were the most powerful body in the community and formed the local senate, or *ordo*. They were, nominally at least, 100 in number, and consisted largely of men who had held magistracies. Every four years the *duoviri iure dicundo* bore the special title of *quinquennales*, and it was their duty as censors to fill vacancies that occurred in the *ordo*. Their choice was restricted by a property qualification (we do not know what it was in Britain), but in the military colonies many of the decurions would be retired centurions. Finally, in addition to the officers mentioned, there were six *seviri Augustales*, who were not necessarily free-born, appointed as priests of the state religion.

Now as the *coloniae* consisted largely of people who were already Roman citizens, constitutions of this kind might be expected in them. But the Roman system went further and recognised similar organs of local government for the native Britons. Such local authorities, or *civitates*, as theRomans called them, alrea dy existed in Gau'l and the organisation of Britain seems to have been carried out in the light of experience gained there. Where possible the new arrangement followed the lines of pre-Roman tribal divisions; the Atrebates, for instance, and the Catuvellauni, emerge as Roman *civitates*. But because of the backwardness of Britain it sometimes happened that no suitable local unit existed and artificial groupings seem to have been made for administrative convenience. Such are the Belgae, which was originally the name of a people, not of a tribe; the Cantiaci, the people who inhabited Kent; and the Regnenses, the 'people of the kingdom' (of Cogidubnus). But in all cases the same thing happened; the local British notables and men of substance became decurions and magistrates in their own cities.

The main distinction, then, between the purely Roman settlements or *coloniae* and the British tribal communities was that the people in the former held full Roman citizenship, with its privileges, while those in the latter did not. But even this distinction is not clear cut. There was another class of town, the *municipium*, which was similar to the *colonia* except that the title was normally conferred on a pre-existing settlement. Tacitus refers to Verulamium, the cantonal capital of the Catuvellauni, as a *municipium*. It is possible that he was using the word anachronistically or even, as we sometimes use the word city, as a synonym for town; but as he has just used *colonia* in a technical sense and with specific reference to the particular period, there is a real possibility that already in the first century Verulamium held the title. Certainly, as we have seen, the Catuvellauni were of all the Britons the people most likely to qualify for it. Later, there is evidence from a military diploma or discharge certificate, where a soldier's *origo* is given not as *Coritanus* but as *Ratis* (the form normally used for a *municipium*), suggesting that Ratae (Leicester) also attained this rank. In any case all real distinctions were swept away in 212 when Caracalla, by his *Constitutio Antoniniana*, extended Roman citizenship to all freeborn pro-vincials; though even after that some towns still sought and obtained the title of *municipium* or *colonia*, just as some of our towns still covet the empty title of city.

Between the *coloniae* and the native *civitates*, however, there was another difference, which is reflected in a verbal anomaly. *Colonia* and *municipium* are precise Latin terms, and as applied to a town they define its rank and the status of its citizens. The term 'cantonal capital', on the other hand, is not precise, for it has no Latin equivalent. The reason for this is that to the Roman, reared in the traditions of the Mediterranean city state, the country was an adjunct of the town, not the town of the country. *Coloniae* and *municipia* had territory attributed to them, but the significant unit was the *colonia* or *municipium* itself, not the territory by which it was surrounded—as though we should think of Norfolk as the territory of Norwich, rather than of Norwich as the county town of Norfolk. This concept also lay behind the system of *civitates* in Gaul and Britain, so that Winchester, Venta Belgarum, in a sense *became* the *Civitas Belgarum*. The extent to which Gaul was assimilated to this idea is shown by the fact that the modern names of the Gaulish cantonal capitals are derived from the Roman names of the tribes, not the individual names of the towns; so Durocortorum Remorum has become Rheims, Lutetia Parisiorum Paris, and so on. How far Britain lagged behind it is difficult to determine; in view of the entirely different character of the barbarian invasions in the two countries, the

3

absence of similar name-survivals may mean very little. Certainly conformity was not achieved overnight and for the first part of the Roman occupation at least, when the trend was entirely centripetal, it is more realistic to regard these towns as centres of tribal areas rather than the areas as adjuncts to the towns.

Below the level of the *civitas* there were also two other administrative units, the *vicus* and the *pagus*. The *vicus* was the lowest class of town to which powers of government were granted, and the term had a wide range of application. The city of Rome itself was divided into *vici*; *vicus* was the rank normally given to the settlements of traders and camp followers which regularly grew up outside forts, in Britain as elsewhere; and it was also the rank of Petuaria, the chief town (or perhaps one of the four chief towns) of the Parisi of East Yorkshire. *Vici* had their councils, but their magistrates were normally only two in number; Petuaria is unusual, though not unique, in having *aediles* as well as *magistri*. The *pagus*, on the other hand—though here too there is a wide variety of usage—was not a town but the unit in which the inhabitants of an area were grouped. In Gaul the term is regularly used for the territorial subdivisions of a *civitas*, and although there is no direct evidence for this in Britain it is morally certain that the British *civitates* were similarly divided.

It is difficult to find modern analogies, let alone equivalents, for these different classes of community. From some points of view we may regard the *civitas* as the county, with the county town, the *vicus* as a borough or urban district, and the *pagus* as a rural district. On the other hand, the situation was not immutably fixed; just as the *civitas* might hope to graduate as a *municipium*, so also the *vicus*, and even the *pagus*, might in due course become a *civitas*. Some possible cases of this change of status are discussed further in Chapter 6.

The apex of the administrative system was the provincial council (*concilium provinciae*), to which all the *civitates* sent representatives. Its functions were largely formal and it was responsible for maintaining the state religion at the provincial level, meeting annually to sacrifice at the temple of Claudius at Camulodunum. But it was also useful to the Roman government as a sounding-board of provincial feeling and it was sometimes permitted to criticise a governor direct to the Emperor. Through it the provincials could retain a Roman senator as *patronus* to watch their interests in Rome; we know of two such *patroni* of Britain. The council had its own establishment—we have a dedication by a *servus provinciae* from London—and handled some of its own finances. Direct evidence on this point is again lacking in Britain, but we know that the equivalent *Concilium Galliarum* in Gaul had a considerable income.

The political structure outlined above remained essentially the same throughout the four hundred odd years of Roman rule, and most of the modifications to it concerned the position of the province as a whole rather than its constituent parts. At some time about the beginning of the third century Septimius Severus divided Britain into two provinces, Britannia Superior and Britannia Inferior, but the reason for the division had little to do with the Britons. When Severus fought his way to the throne he had to overcome two rivals, Clodius Albinus, the governor of Britain, and Pescennius Niger, the governor of Syria. Both commanded large armies and to guard against a repetition of such a threat Severus adopted the same course in both cases; Syria too was divided into two provinces. From 259 to 274 Britain, together with Gaul and Spain, formed a part of the separate Gallic Empire under Postumus, Victorinus and the Tetrici, but it was still a Roman Empire in conception and the effect on Britain was slight; and the same is true of Britain's nine years of independence under Carausius and Allectus.

After the defeat of Allectus, in 296, Britain became subject to the sweeping reforms introduced by Diocletian. These separated the military from the civil governorship and divided the country into four provinces—Britannia Prima, Britannia Secunda, Maxima Caesariensis and Flavia Caesariensis; and a fifth, Valentia, appears later in the *Notitia* and Ammianus. The whole of Britain now ranked as a Diocese, but even its civil governor, called a *Vicarius*, was not directly responsible to the Emperor but to the Praetorian Prefect of Gaul, who presided as a sort of Viceroy at Trier. But Diocletian was also responsible for a number of more detailed reforms, including some which aimed at making various occupations, and even the office of decurion, hereditary, and the background to these, so far as it concerns Britain, requires consideration.

The introduction of the Roman system of local government into Britain had not represented a social revolution. As we have seen, Celtic society was itself oligarchic and although the titles were new the relations between the former Celtic *equites* and their inferiors remained unchanged. The first generation of decurions must have felt keenly the denial of their hereditary right to lead their people to war as and when they pleased, as they also resented the demands for supplies for the Roman army, but administrative duties were not new to them and they were as interested as the Romans in the maintenance of public order. Under Roman rule their status was guaranteed, and ·magistrates were granted Roman citizenship. While they were responsible for the collection of taxes, in cash and in kind, they also had some say in the assessment on which the taxes were based and could levy their own, local, taxes. While they were required to finance, or at least to underwrite, public expenditure, they also controlled their canton's finances and public property. They were not paid for their duties, because they did not need to be. The agricultural wealth of the country was in their hands and provided stability was maintained, and the demands of the central government were not excessive, they could recover from the most lavish expenditure on buildings or public spectacles.

Unfortunately these conditions could not prevail indefinitely. In the first place the introduction of Roman ways must have created tensions in British society. Under the old regime the position of the aristocracy was simple, combining wealth with power. Under the new, not only was their power curtailed by the imperial government but they were deprived of their traditional means of increasing their wealth. While in theory for a man who held Roman citizenship a provincial origin was no bar to his attaining the highest positions in the Empire, Britain, unlike Gaul and Spain, produced few imperial figures. So far as wealth was concerned, the improved communications and the imposition of peace gave a great impetus to trade and industry, and these were not the exclusive preserve of the old aristocracy. In them citizens and *peregrini* and freedmen could all take part, and it is perhaps not irrelevant to recall that the most influential British merchant whose name we know, M. Aurelius Lunaris, was probably a freedman. With money so acquired land could be bought and mortgages offered and in time new men could supplant the old. Nor are we dealing only with Britons. We have no means of telling how much foreign blood and foreign capital flowed into Britain in the wake of the legions, but it is certain that there was a good deal of it. Dio cites as one of the causes of the Boudiccan revolt the abrupt withdrawal by Seneca of his enormous loans to the Britons, and the merchants whom Tacitus describes as thronging London at the same period must have come largely from overseas. And though its operation may have been slow, the maxim *'ubicunque Romanus vicit habitat'* did not apply only to military colonies.

But there were deeper forces at work which affected new men and old alike. Being based on slavery, Roman society had no incentive to develop new productive techniques and the economic progress of the Empire depended in the main on two things: improvements in organisation and the acquisition of additional wealth, both material and human, by conquest. In Britain the organisation took the form of releasing the productive energies of the warring tribes by enforcing peace. That Britain benefited thereby is shown by a marked improvement in the living conditions of at least a section of the population, but against it had to be set the expense of maintaining defensive forces in Wales and the north, and in any event the effect was not cumulative. The expansion of the Empire, and with it the acquisition of new wealth, came to an end in the second century and from that time onward the economic decline set in.

The economic difficulties were exacerbated by a succession of civil wars. The long period of internal peace which had begun with the accession of Vespasian in A.D. 69 was broken in 192 by the assassination of Commodus and the struggle for the throne in which Septimius Severus emerged triumphant. Severus succeeded in restoring order for a time, but throughout the third and fourth centuries the Roman armies were as often engaged with each other as with the Empire's external enemies. These civil wars were doubly expensive, as the maintenance of both sides fell upon the Empire, and whichever triumphed the provinces lost. To pay for them heavier and heavier contributions were demanded from the cities and the individuals who represented them. In these circumstances the offices of decurion and magistrate became a burden, and although spending on civic luxuries was cut to the bone the responsibility for taxes became almost intolerable. As the landowners turned the screw on their tenants, more and more of these left their holdings and took to brigandage, contributing their quota to the bands of marauders known in Gaul as *bagaudae*. Despite Diocletian's efforts to restore the situation by a rigid code of duties, the solid basis of society began to disintegrate and it was against a demoralised empire that the final barbarian assaults were launched.

This process of decline is a matter of imperial history, but for the details of its stages we have hitherto had to rely on the accounts of the literary historians. This has inevitably restricted our knowledge, particularly because the best of them was writing of contemporary events. While it is not at all true that Ammianus deals only with court scandal, it is true that he concerns himself (very properly) with what he considered to be the main stream of events; and while he does not try to conceal his political preferences behind a façade of independence, the mere recognition of them does not give us the other side of the story. Nor should we have it if we had seven Ammiani, each writing from a different point of view. What is wanting is economic evidence, and no Roman historian ever published statistical appendices. We can, however, partly supply the lack from archaeology, and by this means we can hope better to understand how far the decline implied in the writings of Ammianus and others was objective and how far subjective; how far, in fact, the weakening of the Empire was brought about by inexorable economic forces and how far by a failure of nerve. That the two kinds of evidence, the literary and the archaeological, may sometimes conflict need not surprise us. It is unlikely that an historian of the future, whose only evidence consisted of letters to the press about taxes and teddy boys, would realise that in the twentieth century this country enjoyed more widespread material comfort and better public order than ever before.

The contribution which Roman Britain can make to the solution of this problem is great, mainly because of the advanced state of British archaeological research, but it must be stressed that Britain is a special case and what applies here does not necessarily apply also on the continent. Even in Roman times our moat was some defence against infection and the hand of war. Britain had her barbarian raids, but nothing, at least before 367, to compare with the waves of barbarians which at times washed over the Rhine frontier. Even her very backwardness was an advantage; compared with those of Gaul, the towns of Roman Britain were little better than villages and her villas mere farmsteads, and because they were closer to the soil they were less sensitive to economic dislocation. Nevertheless, when all this has been said, it is still a matter of some historical importance that recent archaeological research has indicated that in Britain, both in the countryside and even in the towns, the fourth century was a time not of desolation but of positive economic development. What would be revealed by a comparable investigation of the towns and villas of Gaul we can only guess.

In any case, whatever the economic weather, the forms of administration were maintained, and, compulsorily or not, the decurions continued to function. Calpurnius, for example, the father of St. Patrick, was a decurion as well as a deacon. And to the very end the *civitates* of Britain survived. It was to them that Honorius issued his rescript that they should arrange for their own defence, and it was from them that there went to Aetius in 448 the last expiring gasp of Roman Britain, 'the groans of the Britons'.

BIBLIOGRAPHY
See works cited in Chapter 1 (all sections), especially:
Cambridge Ancient History, x, xi and xii.
Birley: *Roman Britain and the Roman Army*.
Brogan: *Roman Gaul*.
Haverfield: *The Romanisation of Roman Britain*.
Richmond: *Roman Britain*.
Rostovtzeff: *Social and Economic History of the Roman Empire*.

See also:
On the evolution of the early imperial administration, G. H. Stevenson: *Roman Provincial Administration* (Blackwell, 1939), and on the period between the expeditions of Caesar and the Claudian conquest, C. E. Stevens: 'Britain between the Invasions' in Grimes (ed.): *Aspects of Archaeology* (Edwards, 1951).

For a discussion of the term *Civitas* in its Romano-British context, see J. C. Mann in *Antiquity* xxxiv (1960), 222 *ff*., S. S. Frere in *Antiquity* xxxv (1961), 29 *ff*., and J. C. Mann, *ibid*., pp. 142 *f*.

4

ROMANISATION—TOWNS

The political organisation outlined in the last chapter was not imposed directly upon Celtic Britain, but rather grew up in stages on the Britain that emerged from the campaigns of conquest; on a Britain, that is, whose pattern of settlement was already in process of change. This romanised pattern displays an organic development of its own, and although its point of departure was the natural, native order of things, the key to it is the military, political and technical competence of Rome. The first stage in the Roman occupation was the planting of forts, whose siting, though tactically influenced by nature (as, for instance, in the constant preference for the tongue of land formed by the confluence of two rivers), was determined strategically by the political aspect of the native situation and only secondarily by the natural. At the same time the larger rivers, even when they flowed through tribal territory, were taken as boundaries as much as lines of communication, first Sabrina and Trisantona, later Clota and Bodotria—a concept which is possible only to a centralised administration and which found its ultimate expression in Hadrian's Wall. As the military tide swept north and west, the necessity of maintaining communications led to the construction of the main roads. These were entirely different from the ridgeways used in the Iron Age; they were planned on the grand scale, they knew precisely where they were going, and their effect was at one blow to make a unity out of the several parts of Britain. Then the efficient use of the roads demanded staging camps and posting stations, some of which were planted close to the sites of forts and some not, and so we have a string of settlements along them which are Roman, not native, in origin. These, like the forts before them, also served as collecting stations for taxes in kind and many of them grew into small towns.

Thus the towns of Roman Britain owed their foundation to one

or more of a variety of causes. A few—the colonies of veterans—
were planted as part of a deliberate policy for their own sakes, to
act as a focus of civilisation and a reserve of reliable men, and their
positioning, though not always their local siting, is essentially
military. Also of military origin were those—and their number is
much greater than was formerly realised—which grew out of the
communities of traders who were attracted in the first instance by
the markets provided by the forts and were sufficiently well established not to move forward with the troops when the time came.
Others again represent a movement towards the posting stations,
which sometimes drew off the local native centres, much as some
modern towns have shifted their centres to the vicinity of their
railway stations. Finally some, especially cantonal capitals, were
founded as successors to native centres.

The question of which towns can or cannot be included in this
last category is not so simple as might at first sight appear. In the
first place it is necessary to be quite clear as to what does and does
not constitute evidence for continuity. Isolated finds of pottery or
coins are not decisive. The Britons did not throw away the pottery
they were using and hurry to buy new the moment the legions
landed, and almost any first-century site is likely to yield the odd
'pre-Roman' sherd. British coins certainly continued in the possession of individuals, if not in use as currency, for some time after the
conquest, and are occasionally found in hoards as late as the second
century; here quantity is the best guide—the fact that Irchester has
produced three or four coins of Cunobelin does not prove it a Belgic
centre, but Braughing, which has produced fifty odd, of both
Tasciovanus and Cunobelin, certainly was. Even the clear evidence
of occupation—huts, pits, drainage ditches and so on—is not in
itself sufficient, for in view of the testimony of both Caesar and the
spade to the density of native settlement, at least in the south-east,
it is more likely than not that a native site which was merely a farm
would occasionally be engulfed by urban development.

So far as the cantonal capitals are concerned, where native
centres already existed the Romans naturally used them, but it does
not follow that the new site always coincided exactly with the old.
Whether or not it did so depended on the old site's convenience in
terms of the new order, and especially on how easily it could be tied

into the road system. Thus Ratae Coritanorum (Leicester) appears to have grown up actually on the site of the Belgic settlement and the same is evidently true of Calleva Atrebatum (Silchester), where again there were no natural obstacles; but at Verulamium (St. Albans) the existence of an early fort led to the growth of the Roman town beside, rather than wholly on, the Belgic centre and Noviomagus Regnensium (Chichester) was founded some miles from its Iron Age predecessor at Selsey. The nature of the Belgic occupation which preceded Venta Belgarum (Winchester) and Durovernum Cantiacorum (Canterbury) is still not clear, though its existence is known, but how far the central administration could go in disregarding the old order is shown by the case of Isca Dumnoniorum (Exeter), which had no Iron Age antecedent and was established two counties away from Penwith, the main focus of Dumnonian civilisation.

Where the Roman town succeeded a hill fort a move was inevitable because of its inconvenience and because of the possibility of its use in opposition to Rome. But even here the former consideration was the weightier; the latter was usually met in the first instance simply by slighting the defences of the fort, and it is instructive to note that after such treatment Maiden Castle continued in some sort of occupation up to about A.D. 70, while Durnovaria (Dorchester) was being born—by which time conditions were such that choice rather than compulsion must have dictated the move. Above all it does not follow that because the Romans chose a site as the cantonal capital the neighbouring hill fort was necessarily the tribal capital already. Maiden Castle, as we have seen, was indeed one of the centres of the Durotriges, but there were others—notably Hod Hill (whose status justified the planting of a Roman fort in it), Hengistbury Head (where Durotrigan coins were minted), and Ham Hill (whose district was later to have an independent capital of its own at Ilchester)—and any one of these might have laid equal claim to the distinction. Similarly the camp in Llanmelin Wood may have been the tribal centre of the Silures, but the choice of Caerwent for the cantonal capital of Venta Silurum may also have been influenced by its relationship to the Severn ferry. And the excavation of the hill fort on the Wrekin produced no hint of any activity which, apart from geographical propinquity, would lead

one to recognise in it the ancestor of the booming town of Viroconium Cornoviorum (Wroxeter). In fact Wroxeter is more likely
to have begun as the appendage to an early legionary fortress.

As with the *civitates*, so also with the *pagi*, one would expect the
Romans to use such centres as already existed, but our knowledge
of local organisation both in the Iron Age and in the Roman period
is still very slight. Braughing and Dorchester (Oxon) have already
been cited as examples of minor Belgic centres, and both grew into
Roman towns, but these are exceptional cases. In general the fact
that two or more Roman roads aim at a town rather than simply
passing through it must suggest that the place concerned was already
important when the roads were laid out. But not all roads are necessarily early and the importance may have been due as much to
Roman military activity as to native prestige. Great Chesterford in
Essex, for example, has yielded evidence of Belgic occupation, but
it was also the site of a Roman fort, and while Cunetio (Mildenhall,
Wilts) may have been in some sense the successor to the hill fort at
Forest Hill Farm above it, here too air photographs suggest a
Roman military phase. Nor is the converse proposition, that a town
through which a road passes in a straight line must be secondary to
the road, necessarily true. This is shown by the case of Verulamium,
where we happen to know the town's antecedents, but an even more
striking instance may be quoted, which concerns not indeed the
town itself but the bridge to which it was related. Iron Age settlement on the river Nene was concentrated in the region of Peterborough, but in Roman times, although a considerable village still
existed at Fengate, the main nucleus was transferred up the river to
Durobrivae ('the fort by the bridge') at Water Newton. The move
was clearly determined by the needs of Ermine Street and of these
the chief was a suitable site for the bridge. Yet this bridge, whose
remains have been found, lies in the middle of one of the most
impressively straight Roman road alignments in Britain.

In summary, then, although the siting of Roman towns was
related to the political geography of the preceding period, it was not
bound by it and cannot be used as a reliable guide to it. Iron Age
problems must be dealt with in purely Iron Age terms and it is
unfortunate that excavation, particularly of the smaller towns, has
so far been on too slight a scale to yield much information. But

however much or little it was influenced by the pre-existing pattern, it is still possible to assess the Roman achievement from the economic point of view by considering the later history of the sites adopted. There were some failures. Sorviodunum (Old Sarum) and Vindocladia (Badbury Rings), evidently selected as road centres because of their native importance, failed to develop (for whatever reason) even in the Roman period. Calleva Atrebatum (Silchester) and Braughing, again Iron Age centres, are now of little account, and it is difficult to see any valid connection between Venta Silurum (Caerwent) and Chepstow, or Venta Icenorum (Caister) and Norwich, or Viroconium (Wroxeter) and Shrewsbury. But Colchester, Gloucester, Lincoln and York, Canterbury, Winchester, Chichester, Dorchester and Leicester, Cambridge and Worcester, all revived after the Dark Ages and are still county towns today. The implication of this must surely be that these places, both as administrative centres and as markets, were as well sited as they could be in relation to the agricultural exploitation of Britain not only in Roman conditions but in the conditions that prevailed in the Middle Ages and later; and, as a corollary, that the exploitation of Britain's agricultural wealth in Roman times was neither so limited nor so primitive as we sometimes tend to assume. The pattern is strikingly modern.

So far we have considered the towns as though their foundation were a single act of the imperial government, like the setting up of chessmen. Apart from the *coloniae* this was not so, and much information has come to light in recent years which enables us to trace in outline the process of development. This is not to say that we can always date the stages precisely. In the excavation of any structure, whether it be the wall of a house or the wall of a town, it is inevitably easier to establish a *terminus post quem* than a *terminus ante quem*. What is sealed below the structure must antedate it, but small objects, such as pottery and coins, which are stratigraphically later than it may, particularly when they are found in small quantities, be no more than survivals from the earlier period. There is thus always a possibility that a development may prove to be later than at first sight appears; and this, as we shall see, is especially true of town defences, where a single section can rarely yield a trustworthy answer. Secondly, analogy from one town to another must be used with caution, and it is well to remember that an interval of some fifty years separated the construction of the forums at Verulamium and Viroconium, both of whose dates are precisely known from inscriptions. In one case, however, that of town defences, such analogy is indeed likely to be valid. The construction, or even the remodelling, of town walls was not a matter which was decided locally. It was the prerogative of the imperial government to determine which centres should be defended, and the reasons which led to the walling of one town are likely to have held good for a whole group. But even this would apply only when all of them could be considered equally reliable: in the earliest period we should expect walls only at Camulodunum and here they were not provided.

The delay in walling Camulodunum, and the failure to equip it for its paramilitary role in times of stress, is adversely commented upon by Tacitus. At the same time, in describing the portents which preceded the Boudiccan revolt, he tells us something of what did exist on the site. Already in A.D. 60 there were the temple of Claudius, a senate house and a theatre and, we may assume, civilised living-quarters for the colonists. But as a colony and a model of civilisation Camulodunum was no doubt well in advance of the native centres. London, which he describes as packed with merchants and their wares, must have been little more than the corrugated iron-roofed trading centres that we know in Africa and Asia today, and Verulamium a straggle of shops and shacks along Watling Street, with half the population still living on the Belgic site in Prae Wood. Almost the only evidence we have for Romanity among the Britons themselves at this time comes from Chichester where, in the newly founded capital of the Celtic prince Cogidubnus, continental masons were employed to cut a fulsome dedication to Nero.

Tacitus implies that, like Camulodunum, neither London nor Verulamium had any sort of defence at this time, and in view of the pre-eminence of these places it is likely that the other centres were in a similar case. This need not surprise us, for Boudicca's was not the first revolt among the British tribes. Already in A.D. 47 the Iceni themselves, with some unnamed allies, had risen against the Romans and both the occasion of their rising and the means used to sustain it are significant. The occasion was the disarming of the peoples who lay within the Severn-Trent frontier drawn by Ostorius Scapula (fig. 9), and the means included the construction of earthwork fortifications. This was the very thing that the Romans wished to prevent. As we have already noted, many towns began as appendages to Roman forts, but these forts were regular military posts, manned by loyal troops, and their function was precisely to suppress and control the natives. As our knowledge increases, it is becoming clear that the whole province was at one time studded with them. The pattern that emerges resembles that which has long been known in Wales and southern Scotland, the difference being that in those areas the technique was not successful. For success was only achieved when the garrisons could be withdrawn, the forts dismantled and the local inhabitants be left to settle down to sensible Roman life in towns.

The decision as to when this stage had been reached must have been a delicate one, and a governor like Suetonius Paulinus, intent on further conquests, could easily miscalculate. But this very difficulty underlies the fact that until loyalty to Rome had been conclusively proved the last thing the Britons would be allowed was a fortification that could be used against their masters; the hill forts had not been slighted only to be replaced by more sophisticated strongholds in the plain. Nor did the concept of a town necessarily imply defences. Its bounds would indeed be defined by the *pomerium*, but this might be no more than a slight bank or even a line marked only by boundary stones, and such an arrangement could be considered adequate even when the main approaches were equipped with monumental arches or gates. In contrast to the Iron Age, when tribes or septs required protection against each other, the only threat that would justify town defences under the *pax romana* would be a threat from the enemies of Rome itself.

In these circumstances any evidence for early town defences should have some historical significance. Apart from official posting stations like Hardham and Alfoldean, which are to be related to the construction of Stane Street, the only civilian defences which are securely dated to the first century are earthworks at Verulamium and Silchester, and this should imply that the latter as well as the former had remained loyal during the great revolt. In the middle of the second century, however, the construction of earthwork defences seems to have been much more widespread, including both new and

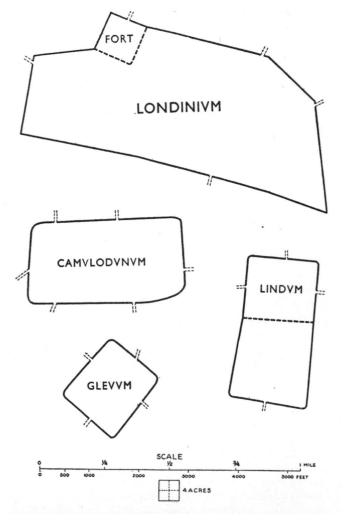

FIG. 2. Outline plans of Roman towns. 1—LONDINIVM and the *Coloniae* —CAMVLODVNVM (Colchester), GLEVVM (Gloucester) and LINDVM (Lincoln). The plan of the *colonia* at EBVRACVM (York) is not known

more extensive works at these two towns and others at such places as Caerwent, Wroxeter, Petuaria, Exeter, Cirencester and Kenchester. By this time, three generations after the conquest, loyalty might be assumed, but the nature of the threat is obscure. In this period it is more likely to have lain in Britain than, as in later times, overseas, and since the towns involved lie largely in the west Mr. John Wacher, who has recently reviewed the evidence, has suggested the possibility of trouble in Wales.

The first century earthworks may reasonably be attributed to the governorship of Petronius Turpilianus, who was entrusted with the pacification of the province after the Icenian revolt. His policy of consolidation was continued by Trebellius Maximus under whom, says Tacitus, the Britons were reconciled to the seductions of civilisation. Thus it is in this period that the romanisation of British life really begins, and that some government backing was given to it may be indicated by the discovery at Silchester, both in the town and at the brickworks at Pamber, of bricks bearing an official Neronian stamp. The main drive, however, came later in the century under Agricola. Tacitus tells us that by rationalising the collection of taxes in kind he restored the good name of peace which, because of the sins of his predecessors, had come to be as much feared by the Britons as war. He had, however, very clear ideas as to how peace should be waged and embarked on a veritable campaign of civilisation. By a combination of compulsion and persuasion, backed by financial assistance, the Britons were led, not to say driven, to build temples, forums and houses in the Roman manner; the sons of the aristocracy were educated in Latin; Roman dress and Roman town life, with its baths and its banquets, became the order of the day. And, poor fools, says Tacitus, they called it civilisation when it was only a part of their slavery.

The reality of Agricola's culture drive is attested from other sources. We learn from Plutarch that about this time Demetrius, a grammarian of Tarsus, was in Britain, and while his account of his experiences makes it clear that some of his time was spent with the army in Scotland it is probable that he was allotted educational duties too; and it is notable that in Britain, unlike Gaul, Celtic never appears as a written language, though numerous graffiti reveal a widespread knowledge of Latin even among artisans. Materially the

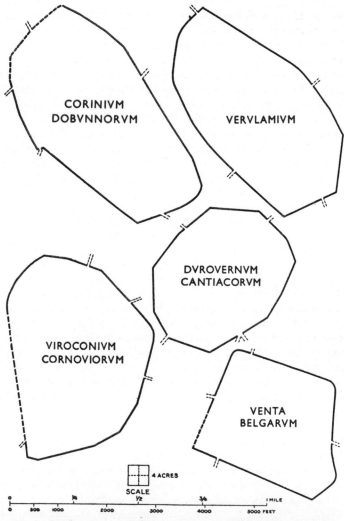

CORINIVM
DOBVNNORVM

VERVLAMIVM

DVROVERNVM
CANTIACORVM

VIROCONIVM
CORNOVIORVM

VENTA
BELGARVM

4 ACRES

SCALE

FIG. 3. Outline plans of Roman towns. 2—The larger Cantonal Capitals—CORINIVM (Cirencester), VERVLAMIVM (St. Albans), VIROCONIVM (Wroxeter), DVROVERNVM (Canterbury) and VENTA BELGARVM (Winchester)

most striking evidence is the inscription, discovered in 1955, from the monumental gateway to the forum at Verulamium whose text, even in its present fragmentary state, enables it to be attributed not only to the governorship of Agricola but, more precisely, to the second half of the year 79. Present indications are that this was, as might be expected, one of the earliest public buildings to be erected in Verulamium, though the temple behind the theatre has also been dated to the late first century. The theatre itself belongs, in its earliest form, to the reign of Hadrian, and it seems probable that for some hundred years Verulamium was in a constant process of development. This was the common experience of most of the towns of the province, and though some certainly started later than others it is in this period that town life in a form acceptable to the Romans was established in Britain.

Our knowledge of the contents and layout of these romanised towns is fullest in the case of the cantonal capitals. These are planned round the forum, which served both as a civic centre and as a market place. A rectangular space, usually gravelled, was enclosed on three sides by a colonnade, along the outside of which were ranged a number of rooms used as offices and shops, and on the fourth side by the *basilica* or town hall, which included the law courts and further offices. On all sides of the forum the town was laid out in a grid of streets, dividing it into rectangular areas known as *insulae* into which were fitted other public buildings, shops and private residences.

Apart from the forum, the public buildings demanded by the Roman way of life were baths, temples, a *mansio* for official travellers, and some place of amusement, and some at least of these appear even in the smaller towns which were not cantonal capitals. The baths served not only for cleanliness but also as centres of social intercourse and they were among the earliest structures to be erected. Often they were built near the middle of the town, at Viroconium (Wroxeter) next to the forum, but at Silchester they were three *insulae* away and there is no hard and fast rule. They were monumentally planned (sometimes, as at Wroxeter and Letocetum (Wall), on a scale which could not be sustained) and were normally approached through a courtyard. From this access was gained to an undressing room and through it to the baths proper,

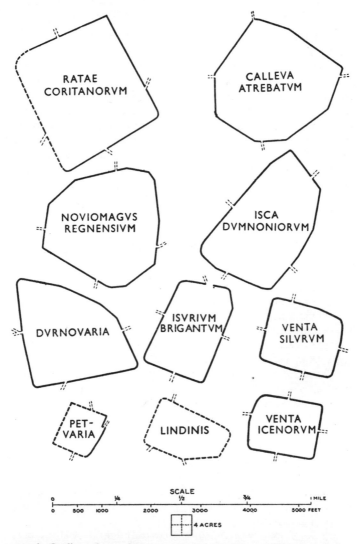

FIG. 4. Outline plans of Roman towns. 3—The smaller Cantonal Capitals—RATAE (Leicester), CALLEVA (Silchester), NOVIOMAGVS REGNENSIVM (Chichester), ISCA DVMNONIORVM (Exeter), DVRNOVARIA (Dorchester), ISVRIVM (Aldborough), VENTA SILVRVM (Caerwent), PETVARIA (Brough on Humber), LINDINIS (Ilchester) and VENTA ICENORVM (Caister St. Edmunds)

consisting of a cold room, a tepid room, a hot room, a sweating chamber and a cold plunge; swimming baths do not occur except in spas like Bath and Buxton and at the probably religious centre at Well, in Yorkshire. Associated with the baths were public lavatories, of which the largest so far discovered in Britain is at Wroxeter.

The temples varied widely in size and character, but the bulk of them were of the Romano-Celtic type. Such a temple consisted of a square central chamber or *cella* (which, to judge by continental survivals, probably rose up like a tower) surrounded by a verandah or *porticus* enclosed either by columns or by half walls with dwarf columns above them. Their roofs were tiled, their walls plastered and painted within and without, and their floors were either concrete or tessellated. Several variations of plan occur—for example, a circular or octagonal lay-out instead of a square, or the addition of an apse, probably to accommodate the cult figure, to one side of the *cella*—but the basic characteristics are constant. The *porticus* is comparatively narrow (occasionally as little as six feet across) and the plan suggests that it served more to isolate the *cella* than to give access to it. No obvious provision was made for congregational worship and while some gathering for festivals was possible in the *temenos* or sacred enclosure which frequently surrounds them, these structures seem in general to have been rather shrines at which vows could be made and paid and individual sacrifices offered.

The *mansio* was an hotel in which officials, including those of the Imperial posting service (*Cursus Publicus*), could be accommodated. That at Silchester, which is the most fully known, was situated near the south gate and consisted of a two-storeyed house built round a courtyard, with its own baths and stables. Apart from the forum complex it was the largest structure in the town—its courtyard measured 148 by 115 feet—and the entrance to it was of a more imposing character than that of any other house. There were also, of course, smaller and unofficial lodging houses, but these are difficult to recognise, though a building at the seaport of Caister by Yarmouth has been identified as a brothel.

Places of public amusement in Roman Britain were of two kinds, theatres and amphitheatres. The Roman theatre was derived from the Greek and consisted of a circular or near-circular *orchestra* which was surrounded for three-quarters of its circumference by

SCALE

4 ACRES

FIG. 5. Outline plans of Roman towns. 4—Other towns—A. DVROBRIVAE (Water Newton), B. Great Chesterford, C. LACTODORVM (Towcester), D. Alchester, Oxon, E. DVROBRIVAE (Rochester), F. MAGNIS (Kenchester), G. Irchester, H. Great Casterton, J. CVNETIO (Mildenhall, Wilts), K. BRAVONIVM (Leintwardine), L. Dorchester, Oxon, M. CAVSENNAE (Ancaster), N. MARGIDVNVM (Car Colston), O. Chesterton, Warwicks, P. MANDVESSEDVM (Mancetter), Q. Horncastle, R. Caistor, Lincs, S. CLAVSENTVM (Bitterne), T. Hardham, V. Alfoldean, W. Iping

rising tiers of seats (the *cavea*) and flanked on the rest by a rectangular stage (*proscaenium*). The remains of three theatres have been
found—at Verulamium, at Gosbeck's Farm near Colchester and at
Canterbury—and the existence of a fourth, at Petuaria (Brough), is
attested by an inscription. In view of the comparative insignificance
of Brough it is certain that more remain to be discovered, but it is
unlikely that they will be found except in the *coloniae*, the cantonal
capitals or London. For the theatre was designed for the presentation of stage plays, or at least pantomimes, and represents a degree
of sophistication. Most towns, as also forts, made do with an amphitheatre, which was designed for shows of a less intellectual nature.
It was a simple structure in which an oval arena was surrounded on
all sides by banks of seats which were interrupted for the entrances,
usually at each end of the long axis. Most Romano-British amphitheatres were constructed of earth banks, on which timber seating
would be erected, but a few stone-built examples occur not only on
military sites, as at Caerleon, but in towns, as at Caerwent. The
Caerwent amphitheatre, which was a late addition, is unusual in
being situated inside the town instead of just outside it, which was the
normal practice. Both theatres and amphitheatres were, by modern
standards, large in relation to the size of the towns. They appear to
have been designed to accommodate the whole population and were
used for more ceremonial meetings as well as for plays and spectacles.

The provision of shows was one of the obligations that rested
on the decurions. Another service they sometimes provided was
a supply of running water. While there are no great works in Britain
like the Pont du Gard, aqueducts of a sort are known at Lincoln,
Dorchester (Dorset), Wroxeter and Leicester, besides those which
served the forts and *vici* at Aesica (on Hadrian's Wall) and Lan-
chester. Of these the most elaborate is that at Lincoln, where the
water was brought from the spring known as Roaring Meg, one and
a quarter miles north-east of the *colonia*, by a sealed pressure pipe-
line. That at Dorchester took the form of an open leat into which
water was led from the Frome at a point some nine miles above the
town and carried along a carefully contoured course to arrive at its
destination at a higher level than its parent stream. For most of
its length it is scheduled as an ancient monument and is still impressively visible, and at Wroxeter, where the Bell Brook was tapped in

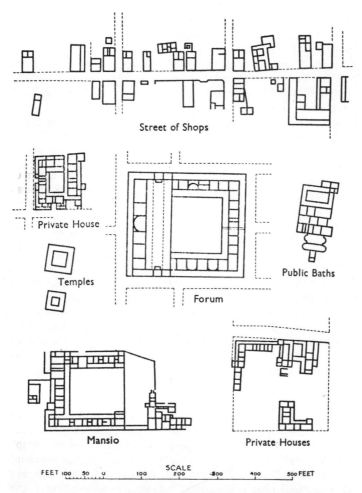

Street of Shops

Private House

Temples

Forum

Public Baths

Mansio

Private Houses

SCALE

FEET 100 50 0   100   200   300   400   500 FEET

FIG. 6. Ground plans of urban buildings (extracted from the plan of
Silchester, *Archaeologia*, LXI, plate lxxxiv)

a similar way, the remains of the dam where the water was drawn off have been identified. Aqueducts of this type involved very accurate surveying and levelling, and that miscalculations could be made is shown by the case of Leicester, where the aqueduct, now represented by the Raw Dykes, seems never to have been finished, and was never used. Here, as in many other towns, water was obtained from the river and from wells. The latter were common in Roman Britain and were very skilfully constructed, being either steined or lined with a timber framework. Finally use might be made of springs rising within the area of the town itself. The best example of this is at Silchester where the surplus water, after provision for the needs of the baths of the *mansio*, was allowed to pass through the walls by a specially constructed sluice gate. Silchester has also yielded the remains of a force pump.

Shops and private residences varied considerably in size and shape. For the former, apart from those which were established in the surrounds of the forum, the commonest plan was a long narrow strip set at right angles to the street. They were frequently constructed of timber, though stone footings are also found, and usually had partitions to separate the actual shop from the living-quarters behind it. In appearance they must have resembled closely the maduka to be seen in the average African town of today, and, like them, were open on to the street. Some buildings of this simple shape, but partitioned throughout, seem to have been houses rather than shops, but the larger houses are normally L-shaped in plan or built round a courtyard. Those of the better quality have rooms heated by hypocausts and some have fine mosaics, though floors of unpatterned tesserae or tiles, or of a hard cement with broken tile in it (*opus signinum*), are the most common. Several houses in Silchester were believed to have had upper storeys, but unambiguous evidence for this is rare, as the staircase would have been of wood. The internal plan of the houses is complex, usually a variant of the bungalow, with long corridors giving access to the individual rooms. While many partition walls have stone footings, a form of cob wall has been noted in several cases at Verulamium and elsewhere, the earth core being plastered and painted on both sides. Window glass, translucent rather than transparent, is not uncommon and inner rooms were lighted by clerestory windows. The best mosaic floors, both geometric and figured, display a pleasing sense of form and colour; the tints of the wall decorations on the other hand are more to the Victorian than the modern taste and some are horrible. Tiled roofs were common, but where suitable material was available stone roofing slabs were also used.

Inside towns where public baths were available, private bath suites are extremely rare. Latrines were normally of the pit type (though Wroxeter, whose aqueduct has been mentioned above, includes some that were flushed with water), and pits were widely used for the disposal of rubbish of all kinds. At Verulamium a systematic approach to the problem of garbage seems to be indicated first by a dump on the outside of the earlier defences and later by the accumulation in the disused theatre.

This is of necessity a generalised picture. Only Silchester has been at all completely excavated, and since the work was carried out at the turn of the century the results are not always satisfactory. Of the other towns, a large area has been cleared at Caerwent (most of it at the same time as Silchester) and at Caister by Norwich (as yet unpublished in full). Verulamium and Wroxeter are still under investigation. In all these cases, with the exception of Verulamium, the very fact that they are almost clear of modern buildings indicates that they are, in a sense, failed towns, and so limits the deductions that can be made from them, and the same applies to the smaller towns, such as Durobrivae (Water Newton), Kenchester and Alchester which are available for total study. It is especially true of Silchester, where the large number of scattered finds in and around Reading suggests that already in Roman times the centre of commercial activity was moving towards its natural site beside the Thames. Roman Silchester has been called a garden city, but, apart from the fact that a number of timber buildings may have been overlooked by the excavators, it is dangerous to transfer its apparently open planning to other sites. Even among those which have been excavated, Caerwent is much more closely built up and so is Verulamium, and air photos suggest that the same is true for parts of Wroxeter. Estimates of population must, therefore, be entirely tentative. For Silchester they range from 2,500 to 7,500, that is, from about twenty-five to seventy-five persons an acre. Towns like Canterbury and Winchester, where opportunities for excavation are more limited, are likely to have approximated to the higher rather than to the lower figure.

In any case neither the size nor the population of the towns was constant. The rate of their growth in the first two centuries is impossible to estimate without very much more careful excavation than was carried out at Silchester. Some indication of a town's area at a given period is afforded by the distribution of burials and industrial works. Except in the case of infants under forty days old, Roman law forbade burial within the city limits and tombs normally lined the roads at the approaches to a town. Thus at Canterbury, if the mound known as Dane John is in fact a Roman barrow (which is not altogether certain), we have evidence that the town originally covered a smaller area than was enclosed within the walls, and in London the cemeteries in Camomile Street and near St. Paul's belong to an early phase. But the law was not always strictly observed in outlying provinces and single burials are not always decisive, particularly when, as was usual in the first two centuries, they consist only of ashes in an urn. For obvious reasons kilns were not normally situated among houses, so that the pottery kiln discovered by Sir Christopher Wren on the site of St. Paul's Cathedral bears out the evidence of the cemetery. In a few cases towns seem to have grown smaller rather than larger. At Silchester the street grid once extended beyond the walls to the outer earthwork which, whatever its exact date, was certainly earlier, and at Kenchester air photographs show the town wall overriding a building of some pretensions.

At or after the end of the second century, however, the process of growth or contraction was temporarily arrested and the situation crystallised by the building of permanent defences. Structurally these consisted of a stone wall with one or more ditches in front of it and behind it an earth or gravel bank, formed from the upcast from the ditch and from material scraped up from the interior. The wall was normally from eight to ten feet in thickness, the core being of mortar rubble, but the material used for facing varied according to locality. Where good local stone was available, as at Exeter, the front of the wall was of simple masonry, and bonding courses of tile were unnecessary. At Silchester, on the other hand, as elsewhere in the south-east, the facing was of mortared flint bonded at intervals with tile courses. Walls of this latter type had a better chance of survival in the Middle Ages, as they were less attractive to stone-robbers, although at Verulamium great ingenuity was shown in extracting the tile which was so favoured by mediaeval builders. In stone country, in towns where the Roman work was not incorporated in the mediaeval town wall, it frequently happens that all that remains is the concrete foundation and a ghost wall—the outline of the trench made by stone-robbers in removing the lower courses.

Where a bank already existed on the chosen line, as at Caerwent and Exeter, it was cut back and the wall inserted into its outer side. Even here, however, the banks were heightened with material scraped up from the inside, and since the original bank had by then acquired a covering of turf, or at least a hard surface, the new work can usually be clearly distinguished from the old in section. This is important, because it is from the make-up of the bank that dating evidence for the erection of the defences is most often obtained. While allowance must be made for exceptional circumstances, such as local rebuilding or cracks in a clay bank (into which small objects like coins might fall), it is obvious that anything incorporated in a bank must normally antedate the bank's construction. On the other hand, since the material for the bank was obtained from an area that might have been occupied for a long time, any earlier artifacts—even palaeolithic hand axes—may be found in it; and as for structures, the very fact that the walls override them must mean that they were already derelict. Thus the *terminus post quem* provided by the odd coin or scrap of pottery is of little real value. Even a considerable quantity of material, if it comes from one area, can be misleading, for it may only mean that the builders made use of an old and disused rubbish dump. Other sections may produce later material, and it is for this reason that in the past twenty years the generally accepted date for Romano-British town defences has advanced three-quarters of a century. From the three sections cut through the defences of Verulamium in the early 1930's the latest piece of evidence was a sherd of Samian pottery of the period 130–50, and in view of the predominantly earlier character of the other finds a date shortly after 130 was postulated; excavations in 1955, however, produced from another part of the bank Samian ware of the Antonine period and Castor ware that is unlikely to be earlier than

A.D. 175, besides a coin of Severus (admittedly not securely stratified) of A.D. 200–1.

At Verulamium a *terminus ante quem* of a sort is provided by the discovery of a hoard of five coins in a repair to the floor of an internal tower attached to the wall. The latest of the coins was one of Severus Alexander (A.D. 227–9) and the hoard should have been buried in the second quarter of the third century. A date not far removed from A.D. 200 therefore seems probable for the construction of the defences of Verulamium, and this suits equally well many of the other towns whose defences have been sampled: among the cantonal capitals Aldborough, Brough, Caerwent, Caister by Norwich, Chichester, Cirencester, Exeter, Leicester, Silchester and Winchester, and among the smaller towns Great Casterton, Towcester and Kenchester.

In considering the various explanations that have been put forward to account for this outburst of defensive work, three points must be borne in mind. First it was emphatically not panic building but represents a deliberate policy; the walls are well constructed and there is little sign of the ruthlessness that characterises some Gallic town walls of a century later. Secondly, if the walls are as nearly contemporary as they appear, their construction implies the existence of a large force of trained masons. Thirdly, although the work must have been sanctioned by the central government it was evidently guided as well as financed by the local authorities; both the size and the shape of the areas walled indicate that everything of any importance at all was included—again a contrast to Gaul. But fourthly, the wholesale walling of the towns of a province was a step unlikely to commend itself to the central government, on both political and economic grounds, without an exceptional reason. A number of events have been suggested as providing such a reason. The first is the northern war, terminating in A.D. 184, in which the Antonine Wall was breached and which is reflected in the south by the deposition of numerous coin hoards. On present evidence this seems likely to be too early for the main bulk of the town-walling, though it may have provided the occasion, on the recommendation of Ulpius Marcellus, for the walling ordinance. Secondly, it has been suggested that Clodius Albinus carried out the walling to ensure the safety of the province while he took troops to the continent to fight for the throne. Here again the date (A.D. 193-7) is a little early, and although Albinus, while recognised as joint Emperor by Severus, could legitimately have issued the ordinance, such an action would imply an unnatural prescience of disaster. When Severus himself came to Britain the disaster had already occurred, but he had enough and too much to cope with in the north: all the forts as far south as York required rebuilding, besides Hadrian's Wall itself. By the time Caracalla succeeded him in 211, however, the situation had been restored and attention could have been directed to more leisurely building in the south. It appears from inscriptions that levies from the southern *civitates* had assisted in the rebuilding of the Wall, and workmen skilled in this type of work were therefore available. Finally, strategic considerations apart, a grant of murage to the cities of the province in which he had won his first victories as sole commander would psychologically be a fitting corollary of Caracalla's grant of citizenship to the whole Empire. But this is conjecture, not authentick history.

Whether the Britons regarded their town walls as a privilege or an imposition, their building certainly involved them in considerable expenditure. Walls were erected not only around the cantonal capitals but around the centres of the *pagi* too; indeed it is becoming clear that every place of any political or commercial importance in Britain was so treated, and in each case the *civitates*, through the decurions, would have had to foot the bill. At the same time, as we have noted above, the economic decline of the whole Empire was setting in, and as the third century proceeded there was an increasing reluctance to spend money on public amenities. This is well illustrated at Verulamium, where the theatre, whose timber stage had been replaced by a stone one shortly after A.D. 200, then fell into disuse and by the end of the century was a ruin. But while civic development, in the monumental sense, certainly came to a stop, it does not follow that there was a complete collapse of town life. The theatre would naturally be the first to go, since it was a luxury and the presentation of shows in it the most easily avoided of all civic responsibilities. As for other public buildings, if they were adequate to their purpose there was no need to add to them; most modern towns would resent the suggestion that they are relapsing into barbarism because their town hall is fifty years old and they no longer build jubilee clock towers. Finally, a peculiar archaeological difficulty arises from the relative scarcity of coins of this period and, as a secondary effect of it, a comparative imprecision in the dating of pottery. As with walls, so with houses, some structures which have been attributed to the end of the second century may in truth belong more properly to the third. It is thus well to be cautious and, while admitting the indications of a lack of maintenance, to with-hold our verdict until the evidence is all in.

The decline, such as it was, was brought to a close in the period following the recovery of Britain for the legitimate emperors by Constantius Chlorus in A.D. 296. Like Severus a century earlier, Constantius had to make good a great deal of damage in the north, and while the legionary fortress at York was rebuilt the forum at Wroxeter was not reconstructed. In the south, however, there was a fresh outbreak of civic building and at Verulamium not only was the theatre repaired and enlarged, but a new triumphal arch was erected. The extent and duration of this revival is not easy to assess, because of the fragmentary nature of the evidence. At Verulamium it was, in the monumental sense, comparatively short-lived, but the wider conclusions drawn from the earlier excavations again require some modification in the light of more recent knowledge. While in the fourth century the theatre again decayed, and finally became a rubbish dump, and a part of the residential quarter fell on evil days, excavation near the centre of the town has now revealed a considerable amount of rebuilding, not only in the fourth but in the fifth century too. Even at Wroxeter, despite the loss of the forum, the public baths continued in use at least until 380, and in a number of less-known towns, such as Dorchester (Dorset) and Ilchester, the predominance of late coins indicates continued activity. But the most striking proof of the recognised importance of the towns in fourth-century Britain lies in the final development of their fortifications, which also belongs to this period.

At some time about the middle of the century the walls of the towns were transformed by the addition of bastions to their outer face. These bastions have for long been known at Caerwent, where excavation in 1925 dated them to a period subsequent to A.D. 333, but more evidence, collected by the late Dr. Philip Corder, has made it clear that the process was almost universal throughout the province. Bastions (or their footings) have been excavated, and a similar date ascribed to them, at Aldborough, Brough, Chichester, Great Casterton and Kenchester, and they are known to have existed, though not yet securely dated, at London, Ancaster, Caistor on the Wolds, Horncastle and Mildenhall (Wilts). Further, the excavations at Great Casterton and elsewhere have shown that a constant feature of the reconstruction was the re-cutting in a distinctive form of the external ditch. The old ditch, lying close to the wall, had perforce to be filled in to provide a foundation for the bastions and the new one, dug further out, was not V-shaped in section like the old but wide and shallow. The reason for this lies in the particular use for which the bastions were designed, to provide a mounting for artillery in the form of *ballistae* or spring guns, the shallow ditch making a death-trap for their targets. Archaeologically it means that any defences, such as those of Dorchester (Oxon), which incorporate both a V-shaped inner and a broad shallow outer ditch, may be presumed to have been remodelled in this way, even when the actual bastions have not been found.

This development reflects the changed circumstances of the Empire as a whole. In the third century the initiative had passed from Rome to the barbarians and raids on the provinces, by sea as well as by land, were becoming commonplace. So far as Britain was concerned, the seaborne threat came first from the Saxons, and it was as admiral of the British fleet, based on Boulogne, that Carausius had the power to challenge the central government and set up his private empire. Carausius was a competent commander, but even so the patrolling of the whole east and south coasts of Britain and the north coast of Gaul could not be completely effective, and there is little doubt that some Saxon pirates effected a landing. Indeed Eutropius (admittedly a hostile witness) even implies that Carausius allowed them to land so that he could catch them laden with the spoils of the very provinces he was appointed to protect. Perhaps as early as Diocletian the seaward defences were placed under a separate commander, with bases extending from Brancaster on the north coast of Norfolk to Portchester in Portsmouth Harbour, and later in the fourth century increased concern at the activities of sea-raiders is shown by the string of signal stations erected along the Yorkshire coast. On the other side of Britain Irish pirates, such as those who carried off St. Patrick, also made their appearance, and there are traces, in the rebuilding of the forts at Cardiff and Caernarvon, of a similar system of defences in the west. On land history had already shown that whenever the garrison of the Wall was depleted raids in force were well within the realms of possibility.

The earlier walls of British towns were no doubt in part a reaction to these threats in their very early stages, but they were essentially a passive defence, directed against an enemy who could be deterred by a show of force; behind them the citizens were secure from any bands of marauders, whether foreign raiders or provincial bandits, who might dare to approach. The bastions, on the other hand, are deliberately military in conception, and the provision of static artillery implies the threat of an enemy who was prepared to come within range and launch a determined assault. They represent, in fact, the strategy of despair that already prevailed on the continent. It was now clear that linear frontiers, even if they could be held, could still be turned, and it became imperial policy to regard towns as strongpoints, which could be defended however high the barbarian tide rose and from which order could be restored when it ebbed. This military role of towns in fourth-century Gaul emerges very clearly from the pages of Ammianus.

Yet even here we have something to suggest the tenacity of town life in Britain. In Gaul most of the town walls, apart from those of the *coloniae*, appear to date from the end of the third or the beginning of the fourth century, and they were built from the first in the new style, with bastions. It is true that their erection followed a period of great devastation, but even so it is notable how ruthlessly military they are in conception. Not only were the remains of tombs and public monuments used as building stone, but the area enclosed was clearly dictated by military, not civil, considerations. In most cases it is very small in relation to the former size of the town, and at Bavai only the old forum is included. In Britain walls attributable to the fourth century in the first instance are rare: Clausentum (Bitterne) and Great Chesterford almost certainly, Cunetio (Mildenhall), Caistor on the Wolds and Horncastle possibly. Of these, the walls of Great Chesterford and Cunetio enclose very respectable areas (37 and 15 acres respectively), and while Clausentum (8), Caistor (8) and Horncastle (7) are very small, it may be noted that Clausentum was a port and Caistor and Horncastle lie not far from a particularly vulperable coast, and all three may have had a specifically military role. What is more interesting is that when bastions were added to walls which already existed no attempt was made anywhere to reduce a town's area. From a purely military angle this would often have been an advantage, for fewer men would have been required for the town's defence and, in view of the labour involved in re-cutting the ditch, it would have meant little extra work. The inference must surely be that there was still, in the middle of the fourth century, a great deal to be protected and men enough to defend it. This conclusion is strengthened by such evidence as we have on the neglected subject of suburban building. Houses at Olga Road, Dorchester (Dorset) and at Barton Farm, Cirencester, for example, both of which lay outside the town walls, have yielded good mosaic pavements in a style that suggests the fourth century.

The last age of the towns in Roman Britain is obscure and archaeologically the final stages are difficult to date for two reasons. Hardly any imperial issues of coinage reached Britain after 395, none after 410, though current stocks, eked out by local imitations, continued in use. Secondly the latest occupation levels, being nearest the top, have been most disturbed and dug into by subsequent activity; this is especially true of towns like London and Canterbury, where some continuity of occupation might be expected. Literary references are not very helpful; when St. Germanus visited Verulamium in 429, the town was clearly occupied, and even a century later Gildas speaks of towns as still in existence. There is at least little evidence of sudden and catastrophic destruction and in most cases the process is likely to have been one of slow decay. Almost entirely cut off from the continent and robbed of a large measure of its trade, the commercial life of the towns ground to a stop; only in the south-west is there any indication of long-continued contact with the world of Gaul and the Mediterranean. Politically, power shifted from the *civitates*, whose vitality had been lowered by the centralised bureaucracy of the later Empire, to the more dynamic leadership first of semi-barbarians from the west and

4

north and then of the Saxons. The Saxons themselves had little use for towns, which played no part in their social organisation, and it was not until commerce with the continent again assumed substantial proportions that the foundations of urban life in Britain were relaid.

BIBLIOGRAPHY

In addition to the general works cited in chapter 1, see also the following on particular subjects:

Military Origins of Towns
G. Webster: 'The Roman Advance under Ostorius Scapula' (*Archaeological Journal*, cxv, 1958).

Town Planning
F. Haverfield: *Ancient Town Planning* (O.U.P., 1913).

Town Defences
J. S. Wacher: 'A Survey of Romano-British Town Defences of the Early and Middle Second Century' (*Archaeological Journal*, cxix, 1962).
P. Corder: 'The Reorganisation of the Defences of Romano-British Towns in the Fourth Century' (*Archaeological Journal*, cxii, 1955). This is valuable for the earlier as well as for the later period.

Theatres
K. M. Kenyon: 'The Roman Theatre at Verulamium' (*Archaeologia*, lxxxiv, 1934).

Romano-Celtic Temples
R. E. M. Wheeler: 'A Romano-Celtic Temple near Harlow, Essex, and a note on the Type' (*Antiquaries Journal*, viii, 1928).

The most comprehensive account of a Romano-British town is G. C. Boon: *Roman Silchester* (Max Parrish, 1957). For bibliography of individual towns see chapter 6.

ROMANISATION—COUNTRYSIDE

Illum non populi fasces, non purpura regum
Flexit et infidos agitans discordia fratres,
Aut coniurato descendens Dacus ab Histro,
Non res Romanae perituraque regna; neque ille
Aut doluit miserans inopem aut invidit habenti.
Quos rami fructus, quos ipsa volentia rura
Sponte tulere sua, carpsit, nec ferrea iura
Insanumque forum aut populi tabularia vidit.

> VIRGIL (first century) commending the life of the
> more than happy countryman to the townsman.

Haec mihi nec procul urbe sita est nec prorsus ad urbem,
Ne patiar turbas utque bonis potiar.
Et quotiens mutare locum fastidia cogunt,
Transeo et alternis rure vel urbe fruor.

> AUSONIUS (fourth century) on his villa, and having
> the best of both worlds.

The development of Romano-British town life, as we have seen, occupied rather more than a century and involved a radical change in British ways. In the countryside the effects of the Roman occupation were equally slow in making themselves felt, but the changes they brought were not so fundamental. Superficially the Roman attitude to barbarians had something in common with that of the Americans, for they saw their way of life as an exportable commodity whose universal application and value were above question. Towns and forums, baths and the toga, were part of everyone's destiny, and they early ceased to snigger at the babu for speaking Latin. But the power of Rome was derived primarily from her better organisation, whether civil or military, and as compared with modern colonising states she lacked two important advantages, a superior religion and a more advanced technique of production.

The accommodating nature of Roman religion, exemplified in Britain as elsewhere by the *interpretatio Romana* (whereby the gods of conquered people were identified with those of Rome and accepted into the pantheon) was in some ways useful, for it made easier the social assimilation of the conquered. But it also conduced to indiscipline, and in the early days of the Empire the Olympian gods had to be supplemented by the institution of the imperial cult, whose symbol in Britain was the temple of Claudius and Rome; and this, as is shown by the tale of the Boudiccan revolt, could be a liability as well as an asset. It was not until the Empire was already in decline that it appropriated to its own uses the truths of Christianity. On the material side, it is perhaps too easy to be impressed by the very real technical advances that were introduced by the Romans. Made roads, bricks and mortar, mass-produced pottery, all these were new to Britain, but in the most important field of all, that of food production, the conquerors were very little in advance of the conquered. Unlike the western powers today, they could offer little in the way of agricultural machinery, and instead of chemical fertilisers they had only farmyard and household refuse, whose use was already common among the Britons. In the unchanging world of the ancients local variations in agricultural practice, such as the British use of deneholes, noted by Pliny, were accepted facts. There were, of course, good husbandry and bad, and writers like Columella were concerned to encourage the former, but in general it was assumed that the local inhabitants knew best how to treat their own land—a reasonable enough proposition, whose application in more recent times would have saved the world a number of dustbowls. Such improvements as accrued to British agriculture from the Roman occupation were incidental rather than direct. Rome did not increase the fertility of the land, but by her system of roads and the enforcement of peace she made more of it accessible and allowed it to be more intensively worked; similarly she did not improve on the Belgic plough, but by organised production and marketing she made it more widely available.

From the point of view of imperial policy the Roman invasion of Britain was a predatory action. The Romans came not to develop the country but to take from it what it already produced. What attracted them most were the metals—*fert Britannia aurum et argentum et alia metalla, pretium victoriae*—and the stamps on lead pigs found in Somerset prove that the lead and silver mines of Mendip were already working under Roman control by A.D. 49. On the agricultural side, the exports of corn and cattle mentioned by Strabo suggest that Britain was able to feed the army of occupation, probably with something over, and it was mainly as suppliers of corn that the Roman procurator had to deal with the British farmers; how they grew it was their own affair. But at the same time the independent merchants dealing in such things as wine and pottery, who have already been mentioned in a Belgic context, were eager to expand the British market and, wherever possible, to encourage a taste for their wares. Thus the romanisation of the countryside normally took the form of an increased use of Roman goods and the adoption of a Roman style of living by people who continued to farm their land in the old way.

Before we consider this 'normal' development, however, some reference must be made to the abnormal areas. These fall naturally into two classes, land alienated for occupation by officially sponsored settlers and land comprehended in the so-called imperial estates. In the first class were the *territoria* attributed to the *coloniae* of veterans at Camulodunum, Glevum and Lindum, and possibly Eburacum, and to these may be added the land given to the Sarmatian veterans who were settled at Bremetennacum (Ribchester) about A.D. 200. It is in connection with such settlements as these, if anywhere, that we might expect to find traces of the rigid Roman system of land division known as centuriation, but no convincing evidence has yet come to light; and in the case of Camulodunum Professor Richmond has argued from Tacitus' account of the way in which the land was taken that the system was not there employed, at any rate in the first instance. In other respects the *coloniae* differed from the majority of British towns in that with them the urban aspect was primary, the rural secondary, and the colonists, though owning and working the plots allotted to them, would be essentially town dwellers. This distinction, however, was probably short-lived, for the sale and inheritance of land, no less than the intermarriage of citizens and local *peregrinae*, must progressively have destroyed any significant difference between the *coloniae* and the rising British *civitates*.

The imperial estates formed a part of the Emperor's patrimony and were administered for him by agents who, like the chief financial officer of the province, were known as procurators. Mines and quarries were frequently included among them, but not invariably so, and there was a great deal of flexibility in their management. Thus in Britain, although there is evidence, again from the stamps on pigs of lead, that the Mendip mines were at one time directly exploited for the Emperor, other pigs bear the names of lessees; and elsewhere in the Empire both communities and private citizens came to own mines. Nor were all metals equally protected; iron in particular is so common that it seems to have been worked freely, sometimes on a small scale by individual villas, and the only evidence of direct government interest in it is the occurrence of tiles bearing the stamp of the British Fleet (*Classis Britannica*) at Bardown and Bodiam in the Sussex Weald. Thus while it must be borne in mind that separately organised, extra-territorial, communities may have existed round the mines, like those of Vipasca in Spain (whose regulations have been preserved), there is as yet no direct evidence for them in Britain; and in any case the areas involved would have been comparatively small.

Agricultural imperial estates, which ranged from large *saltus*, covering hundreds of square miles, to individual farms, are still more elusive and cannot be securely identified without the help of inscriptions. That there were some in Britain is certain—for example, Tacitus tells us that the Icenian king Prasutagus made Nero one of his heirs, and the bequest is hardly likely to have been abandoned after the revolt of Boudicca—but here again the property was not inalienable and in the later Empire it was sometimes leased or sold to private individuals. Even while they remained in the Emperor's hands, the nature of the occupation of the estates differed little from that of other areas. The procurator in charge of a *saltus* might live in some style in a villa, while the bailiff of a smaller unit, who was sometimes a slave, might have to content himself with something humbler; and the degree of farming efficiency, for the reasons already stated, would not be noticeably greater. The distinction between these peculiar areas and the rest of Britain, therefore, was legal rather than material and is unlikely to be detectable by archaeological means alone. At the same time, as will be noticed below, there are areas where certain peculiarities, especially the absence of villas and towns, may best be explained by the supposition that imperial estates existed in them. On the epigraphic side, a hint is provided by the discovery near the villa at Combe Down, Bath, of an inscription recording the restoration of *principia* in the reign of Caracalla.

When we turn to the normal development of the countryside, we are at once faced with a problem of terminology, the core of which is the meaning to be attached to the word 'villa'. Everyone knows that villas are the most characteristic, as they are certainly the most spectacular, of Roman remains in the countryside, and everyone has a fair idea of what he means by a typical Roman villa; it is a house with well-built walls, several rooms, hypocausts, and tessellated pavements, some of them mosaics. But this is only one side of the picture. In the past fifty years increasing stress has been laid on the economic function of these places, and their more refined aspects have been played down. Probably the most widely accepted definition of a villa at the present time is that given by Collingwood in *The Archaeology of Roman Britain*:

'Villa', in Latin, means farm. It is an economic term; it refers to the fact that the place so designated is an agricultural establishment. . . . There is a popular tendency to restrict its application to the country houses of the rich, with luxurious accessories and an ambitious plan; but there is no good reason for any such restriction. Any house of the Roman period may be called a villa, provided it was the dwelling of people, somewhat Romanised in manners, who farmed a plot of land; as opposed to a town house on the one hand and a cottage on the other.

This definition has certain shortcomings, which were recognised by Collingwood himself. Thus in a later chapter in the same work he remarks that 'for practical purposes a division can be made on an *architectural* basis between Roman and native settlements' and distinguishes between 'the type of the villa' and 'the type of the hut'; and of the isolated farms of 'the less Romanised population of Britain' he says that 'in economic character, though not in degree of Romanisation, these establishments resembled villas'. But the problem was made easier for Collingwood by the belief then current that the normal form of native habitation was the village and that the single farm, though not indeed a Roman innovation, was, in its lower forms, a rarity. Now that we realise that single farms were in fact normal among the native population both in the Iron Age and in the Roman period, the economic criterion, as expressed by Collingwood, has lost much of its force. It has indeed been argued that all these native farms should be included in the category of villa, but this would deprive the word of any significant meaning, offend against common usage and, especially in the phrase 'villa system', create confusion. 'Villa' is a Latin word, and we can only be justified in adopting it, in preference to the English word 'farm', if we can apply it to a specifically Roman phenomenon. We must, therefore, consider further the social and historical aspects of the matter.

The formal justification for Collingwood's definition may be found in no less an authority than the Digest, where we are told that just as in towns buildings are called *aedes* and open land *area*, so in the country buildings are *villae* and land *ager*, the whole being comprised in a *fundus*, or farm. But not all rural buildings were *villae*; there were also turf-roofed hovels called *tuguria*, like that of the luckless Meliboeus in the first Eclogue, and cottages or *casae*, the word which Caesar actually uses for the thatched huts of the Gauls. The villa was more than these, in that it was the centre of an estate, some of whose workers might live in *tuguria* or *casae*, and an estate is a developed unit; it is unlikely, for example, that the Corycian man of independent mind in the fourth Georgic would have looked on his small holding, except perhaps ironically, as his villa. At the other end of the scale the term villa was certainly applied to some establishments which were not primarily agricultural, such as those of Hadrian and Pliny the Younger. So far as Britain itself is concerned, the word appears only once, when Villa Faustini is listed as a road-station in the Antonine Itinerary (apparently at Scole, on the borders of Norfolk and Suffolk, where nothing recognisable as a villa has so far been discovered).

Provided, therefore, that we bear in mind the agricultural undertones we may, for our own purposes, restrict the use of 'villa' somewhat and lay rather more stress on the degree of civilisation of the occupant. This has the obvious practical advantage that it erects a standard which will be reflected in the architecture, the appointments and the contents of the house involved, and so can be established archaeologically, but it may also lead us a step further. Although it may be only because any writer had to be something of a townsman to obtain a hearing, it is still true that in literature a villa is usually an estate seen through the townsman's eyes. It was to the townsman that Varro and Virgil and Columella were commending the country and it was townsmen whom they wished to interest in agriculture. We might, therefore, be justified in regarding a villa as a place in the country belonging to someone who was, in feeling if not actually in origin, a town-dweller. His motives for engaging in agriculture might vary, from the hard economic to the Virgilian romantic, but his house would still be, in its appointments, *urbs in rure*. The owner would remain at heart a citizen.

If we accept such a concept, two conclusions follow from it. First, since villa means farm, we cannot have a villa within a town; this is generally agreed, though such a horrid usage does from time to time still occur. But secondly, if a villa is a farm run by, or at any rate for, a townsman, we cannot have a villa without a town. Thus in the first age of Roman Britain, when town life did not exist, villas cannot have existed either—unless, of course, they belonged to citizens of other provinces (for which there is no evidence) or to exceptional people, such as the owner of Fishbourne seems to have been; you cannot be a country gentleman unless you are first a gentleman. And this is more than verbal quibbling. It means that in the first century, and for most of the second, a romanised farm in Britain is likely to represent a different thing, both socially and economically, from what it would in Italy, or in Britain itself at a later period. Any villas in Italy that resulted from Virgil's propaganda represented a centrifugal tendency; in Britain the process of romanisation was centripetal. Further, the development of true villas in Britain in the third and fourth centuries need not, as has sometimes been suggested, mean a failure of romanisation; to Augustus, the architect of the Empire and the patron of Virgil, it might have appeared as its crowning success. The decline comes only when corn-drying ovens are cut through mosaic pavements.

It is only in the last quarter of a century that we have had good archaeological evidence for the earlier stages of the romanisation of the British countryside, and even today there are very few cases in which the first phase has been adequately studied. Leaving aside Fishbourne, where an exotic continental-style villa sprang up within a century of the conquest, the best examples are Lockleys and Park Street, both in Hertfordshire (fig. 7). At Lockleys the first occupation of the site was represented by the remains of a circular hut, some twelve feet in diameter, which, from the Belgic pottery associated with it, was dated to the first quarter of the first century A.D. This was succeeded, at some time before the Claudian conquest, by a second Belgic hut. Though this was larger than the first, the foundations of the later Roman buildings had been dug too deeply into it for any clear idea to be formed as to its plan, but it was evident from the general character of the pottery and the absence of imported wares that the standards of its occupants were not particularly high. After the Roman conquest this Belgic farm continued in occupation, with Roman pottery, including Samian, progressively ousting the local wares, until about A.D. 60–70. At this time a radical change took place and a new house was erected which both in its plan and its materials marks a departure from the native and an adoption of the Roman style. The new plan was rectangular and included five separate rooms, with a verandah, whose roof was supported by timber posts on flint bases, running along the west front. All the walls had well-laid foundations of flint and chalk rubble and above them were constructed of dressed flint and mortar; in the south-east angle at least brick was used. The upper part of the walls—their height is quite uncertain—was probably timber-framed, but they were faced with painted wall-plaster and the made floors, of coarse red tesserae in one room and tiles in others, were probably an original feature. This house continued in use until the second half of the second century, when it was rebuilt and greatly enlarged. The verandah was now replaced by a stone-built corridor and new wings were added at each end, thus converting the plan to that of a 'winged corridor' house. The effect of this remodelling was to more than double the number of rooms and in one case the extension was vertical as well as horizontal. The sloping ground on which the house lay was capitalised by building the north wing in two storeys of which the upper, presumed to be connected with the other rooms by a wooden stair, was five or six feet above, and the lower, which had its own external door, was a similar height below the rest of the house. When the building was destroyed by fire early in the fourth century the floor of the upper room, with the ceiling of the lower, collapsed into the basement and was fortunately not removed when the final rebuilding of the house took place about A.D. 330–40. Of the house that resulted from this final reconstruction too little remained for its plan to be recovered.

At Park Street the occupation of the site went back earlier, and the finds included pottery of the Early Bronze Age and of Iron Age A2. The presence of the former must be due to coincidence, but the latter may indicate that a hut already existed here when the land was taken over by Belgic settlers. In the Belgic period three phases of occupation were distinguished, all dated within the first century A.D. The hut belonging to the first phase appeared, like that at Lockleys, to be round or oval, but in the second phase a rectangular floor, 26 feet long by 10–12 feet broad, was discovered and with it was associated a pit whose contents included the slave chain already referred to; in the third phase, which corresponded to the early years of Roman rule, two rectangular huts, of indeterminate size, were in use. Nevertheless the conversion to Roman standards was hardly less marked than at Lockleys, and about A.D. 65 a new house was erected, almost identical in plan and construction with that already described on the other site. Indeed the only significant differences are the absence here of a verandah (the outlying wall to the south-west appeared to belong to a yard rather than a corridor) and the inclusion at this early stage of a cellar, approached from the outside, at the northern end. Here, too, the house was rebuilt and greatly enlarged about the middle of the second century, and although the plan is somewhat more complicated a relationship to the winged corridor idea is evident. A difference from Lockleys was the presence in one room of a channelled hypocaust, but this appeared to be for drying corn rather than for room heating, and the standard of comfort in the two houses remained very similar. The parallel is continued even in the later phase; at Park Street, as at Lockleys, the second stone-built house continued in use for something like a century, fell into decay, and was finally succeeded by a complete rebuilding early in the fourth century.

It would obviously be premature to take these two examples and assume that a similar process occurred everywhere, but the very close parallel between them does suggest that it was not uncommon, at least in the territory of the Catuvellauni. Further, another example, from the other side of the province, indicates that it was not a purely local phenomenon. At Catsgore near Ilchester, in the canton of the Durotriges, a site excavated by Mr. Ralegh Radford in 1950 revealed a somewhat similar sequence, taking place, as indeed might be expected, a generation later. Here a circular thatched timber hut, some thirty feet in diameter, was occupied from approximately A.D. 70 to A.D. 100, when it was succeeded by two rectangular stone buildings, 46 feet by 24 feet and 40 feet by 22 feet respectively, set at right angles to each other and divided by a passage four feet wide. Here too there appears to have been a period of decay, possibly even of desertion, in the third century, and here also a new building was erected about A.D. 330. While allowing for some elasticity in the time scale it is, therefore, legitimate to treat Park Street and Lockleys as type sites and to make some general deductions from them.

In the first place romanisation was normally a slow, not a sudden, process. In the south-east it began, as we have already noted, before the conquest, and after the conquest it is for some time marked by no more than an increase in the amount of Roman currency and Roman-style pottery in daily use. It is only some twenty years after the conquest—later still in the south-west—that romanisation begins to affect architecture, and when it does so the first buildings are about as simple as they could be while yet justifying the use of the new techniques. This simplicity not only indicates very clearly that the occupants are still Britons, not immigrant land-grabbers, but also suggests that no social revolution is involved. Though roomy enough by modern suburban standards, the houses are not much larger than huts of the Little Woodbury type; and while some Iron Age huts, like that figured from Maiden Castle, are very much smaller, it must be remembered that these were likely to stand in groups, each structure fulfilling the function of a room. The early romanised house pulls all the rooms under one roof, but it does not yet make any clear distinction between master and man; it still suggests the family group, with or without a few slaves, as the working unit. There are modern analogies for this phase. In East Africa, for example, the traditional circular huts have been replaced

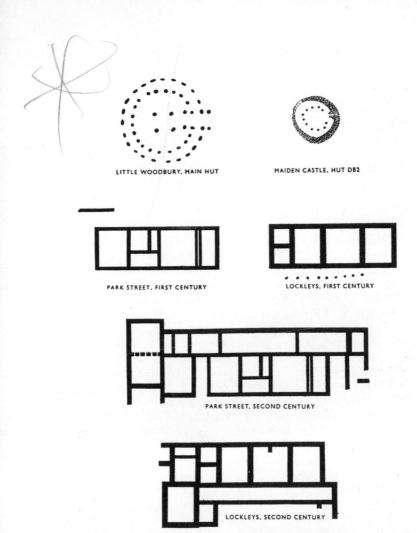

LITTLE WOODBURY, MAIN HUT

MAIDEN CASTLE, HUT DB2

PARK STREET, FIRST CENTURY

LOCKLEYS, FIRST CENTURY

PARK STREET, SECOND CENTURY

LOCKLEYS, SECOND CENTURY

SCALE

FIG. 7. Ground plans of Iron Age huts and Romano-British farm-houses, at the same scale. (Little Woodbury after G. Bersu in *Procs. Prehistoric Society*, VI, Maiden Castle after R. E. M. Wheeler: *Maiden Castle*, Park Street after H. E. O'Neil in *Archaeological Journal*, CII, Lockleys after J. B. Ward Perkins in *Antiquaries Journal*, XVIII)

by new rectangular houses of a simple bungalow type—as it happens very like a simple and small corridor villa. These new houses incorporate such innovations as concrete floors and corrugated-iron roofs; inside they are furnished in European style with tables and chairs, wedding photographs hang on the walls, and European cutlery, crockery and enamelware are increasingly used. But two particular points deserve notice. First, this architectural revolution of itself implies little social change and the system of land tenure, for instance, does not necessarily alter with it. Secondly, the houses that are in fact being simulated are, except in a few cases of rich and powerful men, not directly those of Europeans, and certainly not public buildings, but rather the bungalow homes of Indian traders. Just so in Roman Britain it is probable that in the first century the houses which the British farmers took for their models were not the elaborate structures we usually associate with the classical world but rather the dwellings, perhaps even the shops, of the continental traders, whether Greek or Gaul, who would at that time represent the most civilised element in the towns; and these are the urban buildings which they most closely resemble. This may even be the way in which the idea of the cellar reached Park Street from Gaul. Cellars are not unknown on other sites in Britain—the later example at Lockleys is paralleled, for instance, at Lullingstone—they are common in Belgic Gaul and Tacitus notes their use in free Germany.

With the second-century rebuilding, however, the houses at Park Street and Lockleys fall into conformity with the northern part of the Empire as a whole. The 'winged corridor' plan is the commonest lay-out among the romanised farmhouses not only of Britain but of Belgic Gaul and Roman Germany too. In its simplest and its most usual form it consists of a corridor with four or more rooms behind it and projecting wings at each end. A not infrequent variant is that where the corridor and the wings are duplicated at the rear of the central block, resulting in a letter H-shaped plan (the so-called 'tripartite corridor' type); in another variant, as in the final phase at Ditchley, the corridor is carried right round the wings; and in yet another, as at Atworth, in Wiltshire, the corridor runs along the inner side of two wings set more or less at right angles—an arrangement perhaps foreshadowed at Catsgore. In all these cases, and particularly in that of the 'tripartite corridor' house,

the plan is architecturally a great advance on the earlier forms;
for one thing it implies the presence of clerestory windows to light
the inner rooms. But the social implications are more important
still. In the earlier houses, although we often do not know for
certain where the doors were, it is clear that one room could be
entered only through another room or from the outside. Comfort
and privacy were at a discount, and all the inhabitants were expected
to muck in together. With the addition of the corridor this situation
is radically altered, the rooms devoted to various uses are independently linked and some social differentiation becomes possible.
This last is also reflected in the fact that one or two rooms are
invariably better appointed than the rest, especially those forming
the wings. The more civilised standards of the towns are beginning
to make themselves felt.

Thus far we have dealt with these farms as though the one
building constituted the whole establishment. In the first century
this may sometimes have been the case, though it is worth noting
that in the East African analogy cited above one or more huts of the
more primitive type are sometimes retained to serve as kitchens and
other outbuildings. In the second century, however, we also have
evidence of a much more developed arrangement, and of this the
best example is the site at Ditchley, in Oxfordshire, excavated by
Mr. Ralegh Radford in 1935. Here the pre-Roman element was
lacking, though air photographs (frontispiece) show marks which
suggest that the land may already have been worked from a hut situated some distance from the later house. On the site itself the earliest
occupation began about A.D. 70 and was related to a simple rectangular house of timber. Early in the second century this was replaced by a stone-founded house of winged corridor plan which
continued in use until about 200, when it was destroyed by fire and
not rebuilt until the early years of the fourth century. The interesting
feature of Ditchley is that from the beginning it was surrounded by a
rectangular enclosure, consisting in the first two phases of an earthen
bank, probably surmounted by a fence or hedge, and in the last
phase by a stone wall. The area enclosed was approximately 300
yards square and it is a reasonable supposition that all the structures
relating to the farm were included in it. Apart from the dwelling
house itself, which was set centrally in the northern, and upper, part

of the enclosure, these consisted of a well, placed symmetrically in front of the house, a circular threshing floor, and a range of buildings, larger than the dwelling house and including a granary, which extended right across the southern end of the enclosure; the entrance to the farmyard was apparently through these buildings. Outside the entrance, air photographs indicate a straight drive approaching the farm from the south, bounded on either side by ditches which divided it from what may have been fields but were more probably orchards or gardens.

Ditchley is unusual in its symmetry and its compactness and in the presence of an enclosing bank which, coupled with the excellence of the air photographs, made it comparatively easy to locate the outbuildings. But at many other sites, too, traces have come to light of subsidiary structures, and they must certainly find a place in our generalised picture of a typical romanised farm at the end of the second century. The farmhouse itself is substantial—normally between 50 and 100 feet long—and most often built on the winged corridor plan. Its walls are set on concrete and stone foundations but are half timbered above (this last point, long conjectural, was confirmed in 1933 by the discovery at Hucclecote, near Gloucester, of a piece of wall plaster bearing a drawing of the end-elevation of a house). Inside, the walls are plastered and painted and the floors are of cement or tile or plain unpatterned tesserae. Tiles or stone roofing slabs (the latter especially common in the west country) cover the roof and the windows are sometimes glazed. Apart from the main house there are barns and byres, often of timber, a threshing floor and a well. It is in fact a substantial farmstead and implies a considerable acreage. Nevertheless a number of features which we normally associate with a Roman villa are absent. None of the houses so far described has a hypocaust to heat so much as one room; none (with the possible exception of Park Street) has a mosaic pavement; and none has its own bath house. This is not to say that these features cannot occur in a second-century context— at Lullingstone, for example, the baths are dated to about A.D. 180 —but it is certainly true that they are abnormal and are not to be assumed without very good evidence. Recent research, such as that carried out by Mr. Sheppard Frere at Bignor, in Sussex, suggests that many large houses which have in the past been assumed to be

built all of a piece and to have continued in unbroken occupation
from the first century to the fourth in fact started in a very much
humbler way.

Here again we must consider the social implications and face the
question, who were the occupants of these romanised farms? There
is little doubt that the majority of them were Britons, but the Britons
were not an undifferentiated mass and simply to say that this was the
stage of civilisation now reached by British farmers does not mean
very much. On the one side we can say with certainty that they did
not represent the generality of the peasants; such farms as these are
greatly outnumbered by the more primitive establishments, carrying
on the Iron Age traditions with very little architectural change, to
which we shall return later. But it does not follow from this that they
represented the aristocracy. As we have seen, by the end of the
second century towns were not only established in Britain but had
achieved some degree of refinement. Roman life, the life of the
forum and the public baths, was in full swing, and while we must not
give it too metropolitan a colour—Durnovaria, for instance, must
have been very like Casterbridge—the contrast between the sophistication of the towns and the simplicity of the farms is notable.
Again, although the basis of Iron Age life had been agricultural, the
aristocracy, whether lording it in their hill forts or leading their
retainers in the armies of Cunobelin, were themselves fighters rather
than farmers, and Agricola's cultural campaign had aimed at
making them into townsmen, not yeomen. No doubt these people
owned the farms and drew rents from them, but it is probable that
the actual occupants were bailiffs and tenants, younger sons and
poor relations, in fact a sort of middle class, rather than the decurions themselves.

This question acquires added interest in the light of the subsequent history of the farms. It will have been observed that in all the
examples we have so far considered—Lockleys, Park Street, Catsgore, Ditchley—the third century was a period of decay. The same
phenomenon has been noted at other sites—for example at Lullingstone in Kent and at Saunderton in Buckinghamshire—and while
there are exceptions (notably Llantwit in Glamorgan and Norton
Disney in south-west Lincolnshire, as they are at present interpreted),
it seems to have been very widespread. For the reasons mentioned in

connection with the towns, the dating of events in the third century is not so precise as we could wish, but on the face of it the decline seems to have run *pari passu* with that of the towns; and as with the towns, so also with the farms, the end of the century saw a great revival.

In fact it was much more than a revival, for not only were farms such as we have described rebuilt, and their numbers greatly increased, but a new form of rural establishment now makes its appearance (fig. 8). This fulfils all the requirements we laid down for the true villa and is as sophisticated as the earlier farms were simple. In such houses hypocausts are the rule, not in one room only but in several; mosaic pavements are common, often of high technical and artistic quality; bath suites are de rigueur; and the whole is conceived on a scale and to a standard of comfort that makes a comparison with the Georgian country houses of a much later period not inappropriate. Typically the plan takes the form of ranges of buildings around one or more courtyards, and while this was often achieved by adding to the wings of an earlier corridor house, as seems to be the case at Northleigh, in Oxfordshire, some great houses, such as that at Keynsham, in Somerset, appear to have been entirely new foundations. There is no doubt that in this period the aristocracy not only took an interest in the country but also, whether permanently or not, went to live there.

Important as this conclusion is for the historian, however, the effect on the overall pattern of rural settlement must not be exaggerated. Here two points in particular must be stressed. First, even in the most elaborate houses the economic basis is still apparent. In the majority of cases, those based on agriculture, all the normal appurtenances of a farm—barns, cattle sheds, farm-workers' quarters and so on—are still to be found and are usually incorporated in one or more of the ranges attached to the main house; and for industrially based estates the very large house at Castor, in Northamptonshire, may be taken as an example, overlooking the potters' fields from which it must have drawn its wealth. From this we may conclude that although these may justly be called country houses they were also productive units and not mere pleasure domes. Secondly, the houses that fall into this class are still in the minority. In the present state of our knowledge it is not possible to

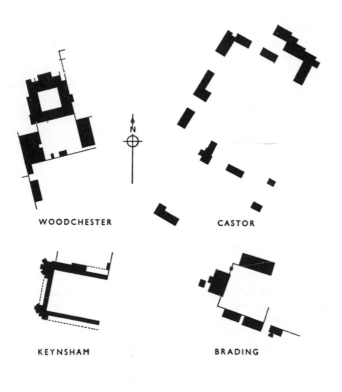

WOODCHESTER   CASTOR

KEYNSHAM   BRADING

SCALE

0 10 20 30 40 50   100   150   200 METRES
0   100   200   300   400   500   600 FEET

FIG. 8. Block plans of Romano-British villas (Woodchester after S. Lysons: *Roman Antiquities at Woodchester*, Castor after E. T. Artis: 'The Durobrivae of Antoninus', Keynsham after A. Bulleid and E. Horne in *Archaeologia*, LXXV, Brading after J. E. and F. G. Hilton Price: *Remains of Roman Buildings at Morton near Brading*)

be dogmatic, but out of a total of some 620 structures which probably represent romanised farms only about seventy-five are really luxurious. Among the rest all degrees of comfort are represented. Thus at Park Street a bath house was added, but at Ditchley none was found and in the circumstances it is reasonably certain that none ever existed; at the bottom of the scale the building at Iwerne, in Dorset, was certainly no more than a workaday farmhouse. Thus we may suppose that while the standards of the town were fully achieved in the houses of the wealthy, they could only partially be imitated by the middle class and had very little effect on the conditions of bailiffs and tenants.

Having considered the main stream of rural romanisation, we must retrace our steps and turn our attention to the other elements in the Romano-British countryside. For, as we have noted, not all farms were romanised, even in the architectural sense, and proper villas were always in the minority. In the first place, on the highland fringes of the province, there were large areas on which the impact of civilisation was very slight indeed. Such are the hinterland of Hadrian's Wall and the greater part of Wales, where Roman rule never seems to have progressed beyond the military stage and rural habitations continued to be purely native in character. Even Roman coins are but rarely found in them and in the absence of adequate dating material their very attribution to this period is still largely conjectural. More surprising is the persistence of Iron Age ways of life in the south-western peninsula, which, though certainly highland, had ample mineral and agricultural resources and a long tradition of contact with the continent. In Penwith the so-called 'courtyard houses', consisting of a number of drystone chambers grouped round an open court, are shown by numerous finds of coins and pottery to have continued in use throughout the period; while in the rest of Cornwall, and in Devon west of the Exe, the only romanised house known is that at Magor Farm, Illogan, and coins and pottery alike indicate an unbroken occupation of Iron Age sites, with Rome's subjects living sometimes, as at Trevelgue Head, within the ancient fortifications, sometimes, as at Milber Down, just outside them. It is possible that a few villas still await discovery— one would expect some, at least, in south Devon—but they are unlikely to be so numerous as to upset Haverfield's conclusion that, broadly speaking, civilisation was confined to the lowland zone.

Within the lowland zone itself, native-type dwellings are widely distributed. A large number are known on the Sussex downs, where they lie above and between the villas; many have been noted in the Thames valley; and several more, observed from the air, await the confirmation of the spade near the Severn. In most cases their occupants were probably either small-holders or dependent tenants (*coloni*) of the larger landlords. In two areas, however, villas are so notably absent, and farms of this more primitive type so plentiful, that some special explanation seems to be demanded.

The first area is the Fenland. Here, because of climatic changes, settlement in the Iron Age was virtually non-existent, but from the late first century onwards evidence of Romano-British occupation is plentiful. There is little doubt that man as well as nature had a hand in the reclamation of the marshes, and the scale of the enterprise would seem to imply governmental interest. It was at one time suggested that some of the Iceni might have been transferred there after the revolt of A.D. 60, but recent research by Dr. Peter Salway indicates that the main movement took place in Hadrianic times. The settlements are simple in character. Most of the houses are of timber and thatch and even where stone buildings occur they are not luxurious; the fields related to them are small and there is no sign of urban development. The second area lies in Wessex and stretches from Dorchester (Dorset) to near Devizes, though its full extent is not certain. Here the Iron Age population was numerous enough, but in Roman times there is a similar lack of sophistication in the farms and the same absence of towns. In both cases the same explanation has been offered, that they were imperial estates, and the theory is made more attractive by the geographical relationship of the two areas to the main centres of military activity. Bread formed the basis of the Roman soldiers' rations, and the maintenance of the corn supply was a constant preoccupation of military commanders. The Fenland was deliberately connected, by the Car Dyke canal and its related waterways, with the legionary fortress at York, while Wessex was conveniently situated to supply the Caerleon command—perhaps under direction from the *principia* at Combe Down. Whether a similar arrangement was made for Chester we cannot as yet tell, but it may be significant that romanised farms and villas are scarce in the territory of the Cornovii as a whole and the nearest example to Chester is at Tyrley, some thirty miles distant.

Even if this interpretation is correct, however, it must be realised that the situation was not unchanging and the subsequent history of the two areas was not identical. In the Fenland, so long as the sea was held at bay, there was no reason why the growing of corn, to which the area was most suited, should not have continued unabated; the contraction of the military demand, resulting from the later policy of encouraging the Wall garrison to grow its own crops, would largely have been offset by an increased market in the towns, especially in the *colonia* at York, and in any case as late as the fourth century British corn was still shipped to the garrison on the Rhine frontier. It was natural rather than economic forces that brought about the decline. At some time in the third century the Fens suffered an inundation which at Welney resulted in the deposition of a band of tidal silt six feet thick, and although occupation was resumed after the disaster it was on a smaller scale than before and had already ceased by the end of the Roman period. In Wessex, on the other hand, there are signs of economic forces at work. The native-type farmstead at Rotherley was abandoned in the late third century, and this fact, together with the occurrence of stock enclosures at Rockbourne and Damerham (and some others which are less certainly of Roman date), and the mention in the *Notitia Dignitatum* of an imperial weaving mill at Winchester, suggested to Collingwood that the Wessex highlands were converted to sheep runs. This may well be so for some parts of them, but perhaps equally significant is the fact that on the fringes of the area, especially around Badbury and in the Andover district, we have an efflorescence of fourth-century villas, suggesting that the imperial treasury may have deemed it politic to sell or lease a part of the domain to private citizens.

From all of this it will be evident that rural settlement in Roman Britain took many forms. At the bottom of the scale were the peasants and herdsmen of the highland regions, whose way of life was little affected by the conquest. Slightly above these were the small tenants and *coloni*, whether responsible to the Emperor or to

private citizens, who came within the orbit of civilisation but benefited little from it. Above these again were the small farmers who,
though perhaps not wholly independent, yet hewed out for themselves a standard of living well above that of their ancestors. Finally,
at the top of the scale were a minority of rich men whose villas gave
them a standard of comfort which was not equalled in Britain until
well after the Norman conquest. But all these people had one thing
in common. They were all, to a greater or less degree, farmers, and
something must be said of the economic basis of their life.

There is little doubt that the economy of all the farms was to
some extent mixed, but for convenience we may consider it under
three main headings: first, arable farming, second, stock raising,
and third, other minor activities. As we have already observed, the
Roman conquest produced no revolutionary changes in British
agriculture. Corn was still dried for storage, but the primitive drying
ovens, as noted at Little Woodbury, were progressively replaced by
properly constructed kilns and sometimes, as at Park Street, by quite
elaborate drying floors; and in the better villas at least the crop was
stored in well-ventilated barns, of which a good example has been
excavated at Lullingstone. Similarly stone-built circular threshing
floors replace the primitive 'working hollows' of the Iron Age. The
pattern of handmills continued to develop, from the beehive shape
to a flattened and thinner form, and imported querns, of Andernach
or Niedermendig lava, are common. These things, however, are
incidental. The main problem of Romano-British agriculture re-
volves around the question of the method of ploughing and the sort
of field used by the native-type farms on the one hand and the
romanised farms and villas on the other.

Direct evidence as to the method of ploughing exists, in the
form of actual ploughshares and coulters, but it is still inadequate as
a basis for any firm conclusions; the most one can say is that while
the marketing, or at any rate the manufacture, of agricultural imple-
ments was to some degree specialised (as evidenced by the hoard of
coulters from Silchester) a variety of types remained in use. The
discovery of additional examples must be a matter of chance, but in
the meantime considerable attention has been given to the question
of the fields themselves. Here the pioneer was Dr. E. C. Curwen,
and as a result of his early work it came to be widely accepted that

native farms (then still considered as villages) used square Celtic fields while villas used long strip fields. More recent research, however, has cast doubt on this belief. On the one hand, as has been made clear, no hard and fast economic line can now be drawn between the native 'village' and the Roman villa, and on the other Dr. Curwen's technical premisses, regarding the relationship of plough type to field form, have been questioned. This is a very large subject—it illustrates admirably the need for the student of Roman Britain to look beyond his immediate period—and here we can do little more than state the nature of the problem.

Agriculturally the landscape of Britain is a palimpsest. A number of different shapes and sizes of fields can be distinguished, and likewise a number of different plough patterns, and the general sequence is not in doubt. The earliest fields are small irregularly shaped plots, often with curvilinear boundaries, which represent the clearance of land primarily for hand-digging; these survive only in upland areas like Dartmoor and can confidently be attributed to the Bronze Age or before. Quite early in the Bronze Age, and increasingly in the Iron Age, there appear the typical 'Celtic' fields, still small but with the straight sides that betray the arrival of the ox-drawn plough; fields of this type certainly continued in use in the Roman period, at least in some areas. In the Middle Ages, under the 'open field' system, the characteristic field pattern was one of long narrow strips which were ploughed, mainly to facilitate drainage, in broad ridges. The use of this 'broad rig' continued at least until the seventeenth century, and the strips themselves until the Enclosure Acts of 1760-1844, when the main outlines of our modern fields were established. Within these new fields, however, a ridging technique was still sometimes used, though the ridges were now narrower. In the nineteenth century the advent of steam ploughing enabled a greater depth of soil to be turned, and while this resulted in a number of new archaeological discoveries it also hastened the destruction of evidence of earlier cultivation. Now the use of the tractor, which combines the tirelessness of the steam engine with the mobility of an animal team, encourages the enlargement of fields, while modern cropping methods introduce a further complication in the characteristic pattern, resembling the back of an envelope, which is familiar to all who study air photographs.

Because of all this development the evidence for the fields in use in Roman times is partly confused and partly obliterated. The recovery of field outlines depends on the nature of their boundaries and these may take the form either of banks or of ditches, with or without fences or hedges. The former survive especially on sloping ground, where they form lynchets, but may sometimes be seen from the air, if only as parch marks, on reasonably flat land too; the latter appear on air photographs as crop marks in modern fields which have been ploughed and sown, but only where the ploughing has not been carried as deep as the bottom of the original ditches. They are best seen in the Fens, but there two factors have combined to aid their preservation; the ditches must have been unusually deep to assist drainage, and the cyclic formation and disintegration of peat has protected them from destruction. Hence it is not surprising that the distribution of known 'Celtic' fields, as shown on the map of Roman Britain, is confined to uplands on the one hand and fenlands on the other. But it is no more reasonable to suppose that this represents their total extent than it would be to assume that the staircases of strips which adorn so many of our hillsides represent the total agricultural effort of the Middle Ages. In fact the reverse may be the case and as with the latter so with the former the hillside fields may be marginal rather than central in the contemporary economy—an idea which is strongly supported both by the distribution of Roman villas and by the present use of the land.

This does not, however, tell us what sort of fields there were in the more favoured part of the country, and the only positive evidence so far available is equivocal. The case of Ditchley has already been mentioned; at Little Milton (also in Oxfordshire) and at Langton (in the East Riding of Yorkshire), ditched fields apparently associated with romanised buildings have also been noted, but in neither case were they particularly long or strip-like and in neither case has their precise relationship to the farm, in its romanised phase, been established. Nor do the upland fields themselves give very much help. In parts of Wessex some of the Celtic fields have been ploughed with a ridging technique and in a few cases the ridges ride over the earlier field boundaries, thus throwing two fields into one, but it does not follow that this took place in Roman times. The modern reader needs no reminder of the expansion of agricultural activity which a national crisis can produce. It was the same in the time of the Napoleonic Wars and evidence is accumulating that in the Middle Ages too, for one reason or another, ploughing was sometimes carried on in the outfield, beyond the limits of the recognised arable. On such occasions as these it would not be worth anyone's while to attempt the destruction of the major lynchets, and so the Celtic field pattern, even if slightly modified, would survive; and this applies in whatever period the fields were ploughed.

There is, therefore, no definite evidence for strip fields in Roman Britain, and in fact their use is not altogether likely. The size of the mediaeval strip, like the Celtic field before it, was theoretically based on the area which one team of oxen could conveniently plough in a day. But the owner of a large establishment like a villa was not bound by such a consideration. If he went in for corn production in a really big way he could, if he wished, use more than one team in a field—a practice as old as Homer, as we know from the description of the shield of Achilles. It is more probable that, like Columella, the villa owners preferred free tenants to direct slave labour, in which case the fields would be associated not directly with the villas themselves but with their dependent farms. Some villas, like Lullingstone and Ditchley, had large barns and some, like Hambleden, many corn-drying kilns, but the corn that was treated and stored in them was probably brought in as a tithe by hard-working tenants, and in that case it is as likely as not that the fields involved were of the well-established 'Celtic' type.

There is no doubt that arable farming loomed large in Roman Britain; apart from the farmers themselves, the towns, the potteries, the mines and the armed forces all had to be fed, and Ammianus (though not Zosimus, who also mentions the incident) speaks of Julian's transportation of corn to the Rhineland as normal (*sueta*). But the maintenance of the corn supply, the *annona*, was traditionally a state concern and while this did not mean that a fair price might not be obtained for it, it did prevent profiteering. There were no fortunes to be made in British cereals, and it would be misleading to suggest that the wealth of the great villas depended on them. It is, indeed, unlikely that any form of farming produced all the luxury of the largest establishments, whose owners must have had their fingers in many pies, but to discover the most profitable lines we must turn to our second category, that of stock raising.

Cattle appear second in Strabo's list of exports from pre-Roman Britain. The archaeological evidence suggests that they were reared in large numbers in the highland zone, particularly in the south-west, where the peculiar 'hill-slope forts' seem to have been specially adapted to their handling, but their bones occur frequently on Iron Age sites in the lowlands too and they were evidently an important element in the economy. This is equally true of the Roman period, when the smallish short-horned *bos longifrons*, a breed originally introduced in the Late Bronze Age, is still much in evidence, along with occasional larger crossbred beasts. Apart from their value as food (whether meat and dripping or milk and cheese) and as draught animals, they were useful for their hides, their horns, their bones and even, in a small way, as a source of glue. Their commercial attractions, however, must not be overestimated. The introduction of Roman ways would tend to discourage a taste for large meat-eating and Professor Richmond has suggested that hides and lard, both essential to the army, would form an obvious alternative to corn for taxation in kind.

More interesting from this point of view are sheep and goats. These had been reared in Britain from Neolithic times onwards and had steadily increased in importance as wool replaced plant fibres as the basis of textiles. Since the quality of the threads improved while the size of the animals did not there is little doubt that they were bred primarily for their fleeces. The detailed textile evidence for this statement comes from Denmark, not Britain, but by the end of the Iron Age we have here at Glastonbury a flourishing textile industry which still relied on the turbary sheep (*ovis aries palustris*), a small animal resembling the Soay sheep of today. In Roman times British woollen goods had a reputation throughout the Empire, as is shown by their appearance, alone of British products, in Diocletian's price-fixing edict. This was inscribed in stone in several centres of the Empire, and the text is still being assembled by the collation of fragments found in many different places. The mention of the *birrus Britannicus*, a waterproof cloak said to be made of goat's wool, has long been known, but a fragment of the edict recently discovered in North Africa has added the *tapete Britannicum*, a sort of plaid blanket. State interest in wool is shown by the weaving mill already referred to at Venta (almost certainly to be identified with Venta Belgarum, Winchester) and there was a dye works at Silchester. The bulk of the evidence relates to the fourth century, and it has sometimes been assumed that the woollen industry was a late development. Since its market successes had already been achieved by A.D. 301, when Diocletian's edict was promulgated, this is unlikely. In fact the evidence from Glastonbury, coupled with the absence of Celtic fields from the greater part of the Cotswolds, suggests that in Gloucestershire and Somerset it was already well established by the beginning of the Roman period; the omission of wool from Strabo's list is easily explained by the isolation of the west referred to in chapter 2. No district is richer in large villas than the Cotswolds and although Professor Richmond has shown the so-called 'fulling vats' at Chedworth to be in fact part of a suite of dry-heat baths, wool is more likely than wheat to have been the basis of their prosperity.

Apart from those already mentioned, the most important animals were pigs, horses and donkeys, and dogs. As already noted, the bones of pigs occur on Iron Age sites, though it is not always clear whether they were bred or merely hunted, and in Roman times both their meat and their lard were in demand. In the case of horses, the Romans do seem to have improved the breed, but the stimulus was their military application—stronger than ever in the later Empire when the heavily armed horseman, or cataphract, replaced the legionary foot soldier as the élite of the army. British hunting dogs maintained their reputation. They are referred to by Oppian (c. A.D. 200), by Nemesianus (third century) and by Symmachus (fourth century), who specifically mentions Irish dogs, and from the fourth-century shrine at Lydney in Gloucestershire we have a charming bronze statuette of an Irish wolfhound. Representations of greyhounds appear often on the pottery made at Castor, in Northamptonshire, and in a stone relief from Nettleton Shrub in west Wiltshire, and Claudian (late fourth century) mentions the use of British dogs for bull-baiting.

From dogs we may pass to their prey. Hunting was one of the minor occupations included in our third category. Besides boars, various kinds of deer are portrayed on Castor pottery, on mosaic pavements (as that from East Coker, in Somerset), and in the designs impressed by rollers on ornamental tiles from Ashtead, in Surrey, and their bones and horns are not infrequently found. The author of the life of Gordian in the *Historia Augusta* says that in the painting of the hunt which he staged in the Circus Britons were shown engaged with two hundred *cervi palmati* (possibly elks, but 1,100 other animals were included!), while Caledonian bears were used in the Roman arena as early as the time of Martial. Birds were snared and also reared in the farmyard. Caesar has the curious note that the Britons kept chickens and geese (as also hares) for amusement, but regarded their consumption as tabu; Pliny, on the other hand, mentions the British *cheneros* ('a bit smaller than a goose') with gastronomic enthusiasm. Fishing, both coastal and inland, must have been widely engaged in, and the gathering, packing and transportation of shellfish, especially oysters, reached almost industrial proportions.

On the vegetable side, though it is sometimes difficult to distinguish wild from cultivated varieties, there is archaeological evidence for peas, parsnips, turnips, celery and a number of plants suitable for garnishing and seasoning, and among fruit trees for plums, apples and cherries. Until recently, however, with the honourable exception of Silchester, few sites have been adequately investigated for plant remains, and with modern techniques our knowledge is likely to improve greatly in the future. On the literary side Pliny states that the cherry, having been brought to Rome from Pontus in 74 B.C., had already reached Britain 120 years later, but this does not necessarily mean that the Romans brought it. They do, however, appear to have introduced the grape vine. The *Historia Augusta* includes Britain, along with Gaul and Spain, among the provinces to which Probus, reversing an earlier decree, permitted viticulture and wine-making, but they can never have been of any importance. More valuable would have been natural forests, which not only supported boars and other game but met the constant demand for timber for building, joinery and fuel.

Finally there were a number of minor arts and crafts. Most of these had no more than local significance—every villa, for example, would have had its own forge—but British baskets had found their way to Rome by Juvenal's day and contributed a word (*bascauda*) to the Latin language.

Although most farms would have aimed at being self-supporting in the essentials of life, when once standards rose above subsistence level some system of marketing was demanded. The degree of permanence of markets depended both on the nature of the wares to be exchanged and on the political stability of the area involved. In the free Celtic world most markets were seasonal and usually associated with a shrine, where farmers and merchants from mutually suspicious groups could meet in the peace of the god. In some parts of Roman Britain this sort of arrangement persisted— it is, for example, the most satisfactory explanation of the vast quantities of coins found in the vicinity of the rural shrine at Woodeaton in Oxfordshire—and it still lingers on in the 'pardons' of Brittany. But as trade developed and political control became centralised, first under the Belgae and then under the Romans, the markets tended to become permanently located in the towns, which formed the natural commercial centres; both *Venta* and *Magus*, elements in the names of several Romano-British towns, have this connotation. The higher the standard of living in a villa, the more important this link between town and country would become, so that it is not surprising that the developed villas tend to group themselves round towns (especially Ilchester, Bath, Cirencester and Winchester) or along the main Roman roads. It is true that in Gaul a few enormous estates, such as those at Anthée and Nennig, seem to have aspired to autarky at the higher level, but we have no examples of this in Britain. In any case, even here the cultural aspect of the link would have asserted itself; the British aristocracy, like Ausonius, would wish the joys of the country to be an addition to, not a replacement of, the pleasures of the town. This connection between town and country is important throughout the Roman occupation. In the early stages it largely determined which of the farms became romanised, in the middle period it must have affected the choice of a magnate who wished to develop a farm into a country seat, and finally it must be given due weight when we consider the end of Roman Britain.

The final stages of romanised life in the countryside- are as obscure as the end of the towns. It used to be assumed that barbarian raids, especially the great raid of 367, made civilised life impossible, but evidence has accumulated that this factor, though real, was not decisive. In places as widely separated as Langton in Yorkshire, East Denton in Lincolnshire, Great Casterton in Rutland and Low Ham in Somerset, new buildings were being erected and new mosaic floors put in well after this date. At other sites, as at Lullingstone, occupation continued, though with little of its former splendour, and a similar trend is evident at Brading, where late corn-drying ovens were cut through tessellated pavements. The general inference is that villas continued, with varying fortunes, at least until the end of the fourth century. Thereafter the situation is at present largely a matter for conjecture, for the same archaeological difficulties apply as were outlined at the end of chapter 4. It is certain that the villa owners, whose position depended economically on the towns and roads and socially on the maintenance of Roman law and order, would suffer heavily from the failure of the central government, even without any outside interference. As they declined, so there arose the new class of ruler, the swashbuckling chieftains from the west, who would have had little tenderness either for these survivors of a bygone age or for their goods and who, if we are to believe Gildas, cared little for the laws of God or man. It has often been remarked that no case is known where Saxons occupied a Roman villa. In part this was no doubt due to their social organisation, based on the great hall, to which the typical villa was totally unsuited, and to their morbid fear of labyrinths. But it is probable that the overriding reason was that by the time of the main Saxon settlement the villas, cut off from their economic and social basis, had already tumbled into ruin.

BIBLIOGRAPHY
Farms and Villas
In addition to the general works listed in chapter 1, see especially *Romano-British Villas: Some Current Problems* (Council for British Archaeology, reprinted from *Archaeological News Letter*, VI, 1955). This is the report of a conference organised by the Council for British Archaeology and includes papers on 'The Distribution of Villas', 'The Problem of Villa Fields', 'The Survival into the Dark Ages', 'Building and Construction Problems', 'Furniture, Furnishings and Fittings', and 'Mosaics'.
The best collection of villa plans is still that in Collingwood: *The*

Archaeology of Roman Britain (Methuen, 1930), and a large number of examples are described and illustrated, with references, in the Victoria County Histories.

Agriculture and Stock-Raising

See especially:

E. C. Curwen: *Plough and Pasture* (Cobbett Press, 1946).

F. G. Payne: 'The Plough in Ancient Britain' (*Archaeological Journal*, CIV, 1947).

R. G. Goodchild: 'T-Shaped Corn-Drying Ovens in Roman Britain' (*Antiquaries Journal*, XXIII, 1943).

J. G. D. Clark: 'Sheep and Swine in the Husbandry of Prehistoric Europe' (*Antiquity*, XXI, 1947).

H. C. Bowen: *Ancient Fields* (British Association, 1961).

Mining Areas

O. Davies: *Roman Mines in Europe* (O.U.P., 1935).

Regional Studies

The Fenland: C. W. Phillips: 'The Fenland Research Committee', in Grimes (ed.): *Aspects of Archaeology* (Edwards, 1951). P. Salway, report forthcoming (Royal Geographical Society).

Penwith: See references given in the bibliography to chapter 2.

Ribchester: I. A. Richmond: 'The Sarmatae, Bremetennacum Veteranorum and the Regio Bremetennacensis' (*Journal of Roman Studies*, XXXV, 1945).

Sussex Downs: G. A. Holleyman in *Antiquity*, IX, 1935, and E. C. Curwen: *Sussex* (County Archaeologies, Methuen, 2nd edn., 1954).

Wessex: C. F. C. Hawkes and S. Piggott: 'Britons, Romans and Saxons round Salisbury and in Cranborne Chase' (*Archaeological Journal*, CIV, 1947).

Wiltshire: C. F. C. Hawkes in *V.C.H. Wilts*, I (ii), forthcoming.

Individual Sites

Ashtead, Surrey: A. W. G. Lowther in *Surrey Archaeological Collns.*, XXXVII, 1927, and XXXVIII, 1929; on tile patterns: A. W. G. Lowther: 'A Study of the Patterns on Roman Flue-tiles and their Distribution' (*Research Papers of the Surrey Archaeological Soc.*, I, 1948).

Atworth, Wilts: R. G. Goodchild and A. Shaw Mellor in *Wilts Archaeological Mag.*, XLIX, 1940–2.

Bignor, Sussex: S. E. Winbolt in *V.C.H. Sussex*, III, 1935, and S. S. Frere in *Journal of Roman Studies*, LIII, 1963, 155.

Brading, I.O.W.: F. Haverfield in *V.C.H. Hants*, I, 1900.

Castor, Northants: E. T. Artis: *The Durobrivae of Antoninus*, 1828.

Catsgore, Somerset: C. A. R. Radford in *Procs. Somerset Archaeological and Nat. Hist. Soc.*, XCVI, 1951.

Chedworth, Glos: C. E. Fox in *Archaeological Journal*, XLIV, 1887; I. A. Richmond in *Trans. Bristol & Glos. Arch. Soc.*, LXXVIII, 1959.

Combe Down, Somerset: F. Haverfield in *V.C.H. Somerset*, I, 1906.

Darenth, Kent: G. Payne in *Archaeologia Cantiana*, XXII, 1896.

Ditchley, Oxon: C. A. R. Radford in *Oxoniensia*, I, 1936.

East Coker, Somerset: F. Haverfield in *V.C.H. Somerset*, I, 1906.

East Denton, Lincs: J. T. Smith in *Archaeological News Letter*, II (12), April 1950, and *Journal of Roman Studies*, XL, 1950.

Fishbourne, Sussex: B. Cunliffe in *Antiquaries Journal*, XLII, 1962, and XLIII, 1963.

Great Casterton, Rutland: P. Corder (ed.): *The Roman Town and Villa at Great Casterton*, I & II (University of Nottingham, 1950 and 1953).

Hambleden, Bucks: A. H. Cocks in *Archaeologia*, LXXI, 1921.

Hucclecote, Glos: E. M. Clifford in *Trans. Bristol and Glos. Archaeological Soc.*, LV, 1933 and LXXX, 1961.

Iwerne, Wilts: C. F. C. Hawkes, S. Piggott and H. St. G. Gray in *Archaeological Journal*, CIV, 1947.

Keynsham, Somerset: A. Bulleid and E. Horne in *Archaeologia*, LXXV, 1926.

Langton, E.R. Yorks: P. Corder and J. L. Kirk: *A Roman Villa at Langton, near Malton* (Yorks Archaeological Soc., 1932).

Little Milton, Oxon: J. K. St. Joseph in *Journal of Roman Studies*, XL, 1950.

Llantwit, Glamorgan: V. E. Nash-Williams in *Archaeologia Cambrensis*, CII, 1953.

Lockleys, Welwyn, Herts: J. B. Ward Perkins in *Antiquaries Journal*, XVIII, 1938.

Low Ham, Somerset: C. A. R. Radford in *Procs. Somerset Archaeological and Nat. Hist. Soc.*, XCII, 1946.

Lullingstone, Kent: G. W. Meates: *Lullingstone Roman Villa* (Heinemann, 1955).

Magor Farm, Illogan, Cornwall: B. St. J. O'Neil in *Journal of the Royal Institute of Cornwall*, XXIV, 1933–6, App. III.

Milber Down, Devon: A. Fox, C. A. R. Radford, E. H. Rogers and A. H. Shorter in *Procs. Devon Archaeological Exploration Soc.*, IV, 1948–52.

Northleigh, Oxon: M. V. Taylor in *V.C.H. Oxon*, I, 1939, and D. N. Riley in *Journal of Roman Studies*, XXXIV, 1944.

5

Norton Disney, Lincs: A. Oswald in *Antiquaries Journal*, XVII, 1937.

Park Street, Herts: H. E. O'Neil in *Archaeological Journal*, CII, 1945; A. D. Saunders in *Archaeological Journal*, CXVIII, 1961.

Rotherley, Wilts: C. F. C. Hawkes and S. Piggott in 'Britons, Romans and Saxons' (*Archaeological Journal*, CIV, 1947).

Saunderton, Bucks: D. Ashcroft in *Records of Bucks*, XIII, 1934–40.

Titsey, Surrey: G. Leveson-Gower in *Surrey Archaeological Collns.*, IV, 1849.

Trevelgue Head, Cornwall; C. K. C. Andrew in *Journal of Roman Studies*, XXX, 1940.

Tyrley, Staffs: T. Pape in *Trans. North Staffs. Field Club*, LXIII, 1928–9.

Well, N.R. Yorks: R. G. Beer: *The Romano-British Baths at Well* (Yorks Archaeological Soc., 1951).

West Coker, Somerset: F. Haverfield in *V.C.H. Somerset*, I, 1906.

Woodchester, Glos: S. Lysons: *Roman Antiquities at Woodchester*, 1797.

Woodeaton, Oxon: R. G. Goodchild and J. R. Kirk in *Oxoniensia*, XIX, 1954.

POLITICAL GEOGRAPHY

It is not yet possible to construct a secure political geography of
Roman Britain, but as the theme of this book is that town and
country show an organic development based on local units, it is
legitimate at least to review what evidence there is and to consider
how far these units can be defined. Three problems are involved:
first, to establish the identity of the units—the *coloniae* and *civitates*
—and the boundaries of the territory attributed to each; second, to
discover the identity and boundaries of the *pagi* into which the
territories of the *civitates* were divided; and thirdly, as a corollary
of this, to consider which, if any, of the minor units ultimately
achieved a higher rank.

For the identity and location of the original *civitates* the basic
authority is Ptolemy's *Geography*. All the 'cities' mentioned by
Ptolemy (he uses the word πόλις, but applies it indiscriminately
to forts and towns) are listed under the names of tribes, but the
reliability of some of his attributions is open to question. Ptolemy
was primarily an astronomer, not a geographer in the modern sense,
and his concern was to fix the countries of the world in their correct
position on the globe; he specifically disclaims any interest in local
detail, which he stigmatises as mere chorography. Since almost all
his ascriptions of cantonal capitals can be checked against other
sources, it is a reasonable assumption that he (or Marinus, from
whom he drew much of his information) had a list of these to work
from; or, perhaps more probably, that he knew them by their full
names, complete with tribal suffix. But he himself indicates that
where he had no astronomical data on which to base a town's
location he triangulated it in by taking its distance (measured along
roads and reduced proportionately) from two other towns of whose
position he was sure. This probably accounts for his strange error
in the positioning of Vinnovium which, although he sites it near the

west coast, must surely be the same as the Vinovia of the *Antonine Itinerary*, the modern Binchester. But it is also curious that Salinae, which Ptolemy attributes to the Catuvellauni and sites near the Wash, is the correct distance from London to coincide with Droitwich, which appears under that name in the *Ravenna Cosmography*; and it is at least possible that places other than cantonal capitals were plotted on his map independently of the tribal names, the latter being simply added in the vicinity of the capitals. This would mean that the tribal attributions of minor places were largely accidental and were made by rule of thumb when the list of coordinates was read off the map; so that the attribution of London to the Cantii and possibly even that of Bath to the Belgae are not so certain as is sometimes assumed. Unfortunately this point cannot be checked by reference to other countries because Ptolemy's methods of presentation, and so presumably the form of his material, vary from one to the other; none of the towns he mentions in Ireland, for example, is attributed to a tribe.

Confirmation of the identity of the cantonal capitals comes from inscriptions, such as those from Caerwent and Wroxeter, and from three written sources—the *Antonine Itinerary*, the *Peutinger Table* and the *Ravenna Cosmography*. These list the names of capitals with tribal suffixes, as 'Calleva Atrebatum'. This was common usage in the 'tribal' parts of the Empire and, as already remarked, most of the Gallic capitals have bequeathed their tribal, not their individual, names to posterity. In Britain the following towns are listed in one or more of these sources in this style:

Calleva Atrebatum	Corinium Dobunnorum
Venta Belgarum	Isca Dumnoniorum
Isurium Brigantum	Venta Icenorum
Durovernum Cantiacorum	Noviomagus Regnensium
Ratae Coritanorum	Venta Silurum;
Viroconium Cornoviorum	

while in the *Antonine Itinerary* Venta Icenorum appears also as Icinos and Noviomagus Regnensium as Regnum. Notable omissions from this list are Verulamium and Durnovaria. The absence of the latter may reflect the division of the Durotriges between Durnovaria and Lindinis, but it may also be due to the unlucky chance that the name does not appear at all in the *Ravenna Cosmography*. The appearance of Verulamium without a tribal suffix in both the *Itinerary* and the *Cosmography* is more interesting, as it supports the view that the place was, as Tacitus calls it, a *municipium*. Petuaria, which is also omitted, is a peculiar case. But, whatever the explanation, the fact that these three examples are not confirmed in the sources mentioned suggests the possibility that the list may still be incomplete; of the other tribes listed by Ptolemy that of the Demetae is the most likely to have ranked as a *civitas*, with its capital at Moridunum (Carmarthen).

The identity and status of all four of the *coloniae* is secured by the mention of all of them as such in inscriptions and in the *Ravenna Cosmography*, though only Camulodunum is called *Colonia* in the *Antonine Itinerary*. Here the most probable addition would be London. Ammianus records the fact that it had acquired the title of Augusta and it appears under that name in the *Notitia Dignitatum*. It was by far the largest, and by virtue of its position the most important, town in the province and so very likely to qualify for the distinction. Both literary and epigraphic evidence is, however, still lacking, and the same is true of two other candidates, Caerleon and Chester, where, as at York, large civil settlements grew up beside the legionary fortresses.

The definition of the boundaries between the *civitates* is more difficult. In a few cases simple geography supplies the answer; for example, the Thames is clearly the northern boundary of the Cantiaci and the Atrebates, the Severn estuary the southern limit of the Silures. A good deal can be deduced from the distribution of Iron Age coins—for example, this suggests the Hampshire Avon as the eastern border of the Durotriges—but it is not always clear how far the prehistoric divisions were perpetuated by the Romans. So far as the Catuvellauni are concerned, Mr. Radford has suggested that it was Roman policy to strip them of their recent acquisitions and confine their jurisdiction to the heartland, and in that case the coins of Tasciovanus would be a more reliable guide than those of his successor Cunobelin. Where coins fail, pottery distribution can sometimes assist, and this applies not only to pre-Roman pottery but also, to a degree which is not yet fully understood, to coarse Roman pottery too. In a very few cases tiles have been found bearing the stamp of a municipal tilery. This is especially so around Gloucester, where the stamp R.P.G. (= Respublica Glevensium) provides some evidence for the extent of the *territorium* attributed to the *colonia*.

A further clue is provided by inscriptions and particularly by milestones. In dealing with the inscriptions of Africa Mommsen pointed out that there, and in northern Italy, the point from which the mileage was measured was related to the seat of the authority responsible for the milestone's erection; ideally that mileages on trunk roads were measured from the provincial capital and those on branch roads from the district capital. As he himself observed, his conclusions cannot be applied dogmatically to the whole Empire, but certain limited deductions can, as Mr. C. E. Stevens has pointed out, be made from them. The Thurmaston milestone, measured 'A Ratis', clearly falls in the territory of the Coritani, whose capital was Leicester (Ratae). If 'R.P.C.D.' on the Kenchester stone means 'Respublica Civitatis Dobunnorum', as is likely, then Kenchester belonged to the Dobunni; and if, as has also been suggested, though perhaps less convincingly, the letters 'A.L.S.' on the Lincoln stone stand for 'A Lindo Segelocum', then Segelocum (Littleborough) probably lay in the territory of Lincoln. On the other hand the inscription 'A Navione' on the milestone from Buxton should indicate that this northern spa was under military government from the fort at Brough (Navio) just as, in the time of Hadrian, distances in Caernarvonshire were measured from the fort at Canovium (Caerhun).

Finally, some indications may be given by the siting of rural temples. It has been observed that in Gaul these sometimes lie on tribal boundaries, and since they provided sanctuary for refugees, places where agreements could be sanctified and markets for inter-tribal commerce, such a situation would be logical. It is, however, a barbarian rather than a Roman arrangement, and temples with pre-Roman antecedents are more likely to conform to it than those of later foundation. A few possible cases, such as those at Frilford and Woodeaton, are noted below, but it must be remembered that there are a number of rural shrines which cannot by any stretch of the imagination be made to fit into this scheme.

The identification of the smaller units depends in the first place on the known existence of a number of walled towns, other than the cantonal capitals, of a character suitable to their being minor administrative centres. Until we know more about the interior of these towns much must remain speculative, though some indications are given by their size and by the grouping of villas round them. Secondly, something can be inferred from our growing knowledge of the political geography of Iron Age Britain. Thirdly, in the case of the Brigantes the names of two *pagi*, the Gabrantovices and the Setantii, appear to be preserved in Ptolemy—the former in the name Portuosus Sinus Gabrantovicum, which he places between the Tees and Flamborough Head, the latter in Portus Setantiorum, somewhere near Fleetwood.

The third question, how far the smaller units were hived off to form separate *civitates*, is more difficult still, and a satisfactory answer can be provided only by inscriptions. So far only one case, that of Ilchester, has been confirmed in this way, but there is at least a probability that there were others. Nennius, for what it is worth, gives us a list of twenty-eight *civitates* in Britain, though some of the names are hopelessly corrupt and it is unlikely that he is any more precise in his terminology than Ptolemy. Here again Stevens has applied the test of milestones and suggested that the status of Carlisle is indicated by the fact that the Middleton milestone gives the distance (fifty-two miles) from it. This argument is made less convincing by the fact that the uninscribed milestone from Scalesceugh, which would have formed one of the same series and was apparently discovered *in situ*, was precisely six Roman miles not from the centre of Carlisle but from the Wall at Stanwix and so seems to indicate military rather than civil jurisdiction. On the other hand the discovery at Durobrivae (Water Newton) of a milestone with the mileage figure I, coupled with the town's size and economic importance, suggests that here we have a likely candidate. The reference in the *Ravenna Cosmography* to a '*civitas quae dicitur Moriduno*' next to Exeter can be dismissed as an example of loose terminology. Archaeologically the only evidence bearing on this question consists in the observation at Alchester in Oxfordshire of a complex of buildings somewhat resembling a forum.

It remains to say something of provincial boundaries within

Britain. The evidence here is very slight. Of the two Severan provinces, Britannia Superior and Britannia Inferior, we know from
inscriptions that Caerleon and Chester were in Superior and York
and Lincoln in Inferior. This represents a logical division of the
military forces into the army of the West (two legions and some
auxiliaries), and the army of the North (one legion and many
auxiliaries), but how it affected the civil part of the province is
obscure. York, as a legionary fortress and a *colonia*, and as containing
the *domus palatina* to which Severus returned to die, was obviously
the capital of Inferior, and it is a reasonable guess that the administrative centre of Superior was at London. A number of suggestions
have been made as to where the boundary ran. The line of Watling
Street, taken literally, is improbable because the road ran through
the territories of both the Catuvellauni and the Cornovii and its
adoption would have involved a gratuitous dislocation of civil
administration. On the other hand, the fact that the Fenland was,
through the Car Dyke canal system, economically tributary to
York, suggests that this area would have been included in Inferior.
A possible arrangement, which takes due account of the road system,
would be one which gave Superior two colonies (Gloucester and
Colchester) and twelve tribal *civitates* (Atrebates, Belgae, Catuvellauni, Cantiaci, Cornovii, Dobunni, Dumnonii, Durotriges, Iceni,
Regnenses, Silures and Trinovantes), and Inferior two colonies
(York and Lincoln) and three tribal *civitates* (Brigantes, Coritani
and Parisi).

Under the system of Diocletian, there is little doubt that London
was the seat of the *Vicarius*: it had its own mint and a *praepositus
thesaurorum*, and Ammianus treats it as the natural place for visiting
emperors to repair to. As to the other provinces, Dr. J. C. Mann has
argued from analogies elsewhere that Maxima Caesariensis, the
first to receive a *consularis* as governor, should also have been
centred on London. There is epigraphic evidence that Cirencester
was in, and probably the capital of, Britannia Prima, so that Flavia
Caesariensis and Britannia Secunda should have been in the north,
controlled from York and probably Lincoln. The British delegation
to the Council of Arles in A.D. 314 did in fact include the bishops of
York and London, a bishop *de civitate colonia Londoniensium* (? for
Lindiniensium) and a priest and deacon from an unnamed city,

presumably Cirencester. The province of Valentia may well have been formed, as Dr. Mann suggests, by a subdivision of the northern two.

It will be clear from what has been said that the evidence for the political geography of the province is inadequate and inconclusive, but it does not follow that the subject itself is a mere historical detail of little interest to the archaeologist. On the contrary, it is central to our understanding of Roman Britain. In this period we are dealing not with primitive 'cultures' but with a highly organised state, not with prehistory but with history. Human dispositions, deliberately made, influenced the course of events as much as the blind forces of nature, and it was the very artificiality of the Roman organisation that made its final collapse so complete. So we may fairly conclude with a brief review of the several political units which made up Roman Britain (fig. 9). This approach is not new—it was that normally adopted by all the older antiquaries from Camden onwards—but since the advent of the great county histories it has largely fallen into disuse. Nevertheless, however tentatively we must draw their boundaries, it is the *civitates* of Britain, not the counties, that provide the framework into which we must cast our material.

LONDINIUM AND THE COLONIAE

Londinium, like its modern successor, owed its greatness to its geographical position. It was sited at the lowest point at which the Thames could be bridged and at the same time made an ideal port for traffic to and from the Continent. Had the growth of the Catuvellaunian empire continued unchecked, it is likely that a Belgic town would have arisen here, but although chance finds of pottery and coins have been made there is no evidence of any substantial pre-Roman settlement. In Roman conditions its rise was inevitable. Already in A.D. 60 it was, according to Tacitus, thronged with continental merchants, shortly afterwards a fort was built at Cripplegate, and it was from London that the main roads of the province radiated.

The circuit of the city wall has never been completely lost and a number of important buildings, including the very large *basilica* underlying Gracechurch Street, have long been known. Excavations since the war on bomb-damaged sites have added substantially to our knowledge and have revealed the presence of a high proportion of timber buildings. In view of the size of the area enclosed within the walls it is not surprising that subsequent suburban development north of the Thames was slight, but across the bridge there was a substantial settlement at Southwark.

The question of the town's status has been discussed above and the unreliability of Ptolemy's attribution of it to the Cantii noted. Tacitus specifically states that it was not founded as a *colonia* and since its importance rested chiefly on commerce there is no reason why any substantial territory should have been attributed to it; the excellence of its communications, both by land and by water, would enable its citizens to draw on any part of the province for supplies. Apart from the early pottery kiln under St. Paul's, referred to in chapter 4, nothing certain is known even of its industries, though a tile works at least must have existed not far away.

Of the *Coloniae*, that at Camulodunum (Colchester) was founded in the governorship of Ostorius Scapula, in the winter of A.D. 48–9, and renewed and strengthened after the Boudiccan revolt of A.D. 61. It lay a short distance to the east of Cunobelin's capital and its dominant feature was the temple of Claudius, the substructure of which survives below the castle keep. There is no conclusive evidence that Camulodunum was ever supplanted as the centre of the imperial cult in Britain and the continuing prosperity of the town is indicated by the large number of mosaic pavements found within its walls. The extent of its *territorium* is unknown, though the small group of villas near Brightlingsea may reasonably be related to it, and it had its own potteries, one of them producing Samian ware, just outside the walls.

Lindum Colonia (Lincoln), founded in the Flavian period in the territory of the Coritani, succeeded the fortress of the Ninth Legion which had been planted, for strategic reasons, at the point where the Jurassic Way crossed the river Witham. In its earliest form the *colonia* occupied the actual site of the legionary fortress, whose defences have been found underlying the walls, and covered an area of forty-one acres. At a later date, however—late enough to allow the use of legionary tombstones as building material—an area of ribbon development down the hill towards the river was also enclosed by walls, thus increasing the town's size to ninety-seven acres. Apart from the possible inclusion of Segelocum

(Littleborough) noted above, the extent of the colony's *territorium* is not known, but even outside the enlarged town there was a certain amount of suburban building, notably a very large house at Greetwell on the east, while to the west there were important potteries.

Glevum (Gloucester) is shown by its name, Colonia Nervia Glevensium, to have been founded in the reign of Nerva (A.D. 96–8). Like Lindum it succeeded the fortress of a legion (probably the Twentieth) and recent excavations indicate that it too occupied the same site. The colonists may have been veterans of the Second Legion, whose permanent base at Isca (Caerleon) had been established twenty years before. Glevum lay in the land of the Dobunni and the allotment of its *territorium* must have involved some eviction of the natives; most of the sites which have yielded the products of its municipal tilery (Barnwood, Hucclecote, Ifold and Dry Hill) had Iron Age antecedents. Neither the tilery itself nor the potteries which produced the early 'Glevum ware' have yet been discovered. There was some suburban building, but nothing comparable with that which led to the enlargement of Lindum, and it has been suggested that Glevum was to a certain extent eclipsed by the growth of the neighbouring tribal centre of Corinium Dobunnorum (Cirencester).

Colonia Eburacensium (York) was also related to a legionary fortress but grew up as its companion, not its successor. Though its walls have not yet been satisfactorily identified its main focus evidently lay south-west of the fortress, on the opposite bank of the Ouse, where numerous remains indicative of a high degree of civilisation have been found, including those of a very large public baths. The date at which the title of *colonia* was conferred is not known and it is not certain that any *territorium* was attributed to it for, as Professor Richmond has pointed out, the honorific grant of the status was not normally accompanied by an allotment of land.

ATREBATES

In Roman times the kingdom ruled over by the Commian dynasty was broken up, the south-eastern part being incorporated in the kingdom of Cogidubnus, the south-western in the *Civitas Belgarum*. Only the northern part, consisting of the whole of Berkshire with parts of Wiltshire, Hampshire and Surrey—mostly, that is, the territory which the Catuvellaunian Cunobelin had conquered—was included in the *Civitas Atrebatum*.

The cantonal capital was at Calleva Atrebatum (Silchester), and this is the only town attributed to the tribe by Ptolemy; but there was also a walled town at Cunetio (Mildenhall), which is mentioned in both the *Antonine Itinerary* and the *Ravenna Cosmography* and was probably the centre of a *pagus*. A settlement has been located at Thatcham, on the road between these two, and the name Spinis, together with the mileage figures of the *Itinerary*, indicates the existence of at least a road station west of it, probably near Woodspeen. The quantity of finds (largely fourth century) from Reading suggest another centre there, possibly originating as the river port of Silchester.

Villas are comparatively scarce round Silchester, but more plentiful round Mildenhall, and there is a notable concentration in the area of Farnham, where there were important potteries and where a town may still await discovery. Rural temples are known at Weycock Hill, at Frilford (possibly marking the boundary with the Dobunni, and (probably) at Lowbury; the building at the Wheatsheaf, halfway between Silchester and Winchester, may have been a temple on the borders of the Atrebates and the Belgae.

BELGAE

The canton of the Belgae appears to have been an artificial creation of the Roman government, including in the east a part of the territory of the pre-Roman Atrebates, and in the west a part of that of the Dobunni, together with the strip of territory in between. It thus covered most of Hampshire (possibly including the Isle of Wight), central Wiltshire, the northern half of Somerset and a small part of southern Gloucestershire.

The eastern part contained the cantonal capital, Venta Belgarum (Winchester), with a port at Clausentum (Bitterne). A small settlement is known at Nursling (possibly Onna) and road stations are mentioned in the *Antonine Itinerary* at Brige, on the road from Winchester to Salisbury, and at Vindomis, between Silchester and Winchester (but with mileages too great to fit the direct route);

neither of these has been identified, but they were probably situated near Broughton and Andover respectively. Villas are numerous in this part of the canton, especially round Winchester, round Andover and in the Isle of Wight, and a pottery industry flourished in the · New Forest.

The chief centre of the western part of the canton was Aquae Sulis (Bath), the most sophisticated town of Britain, where tombstones attest the presence of continental visitors. The port of Bath was at Abonae (Sea Mills), which appears in the *Itinerary* as the eastern terminal of a ferry across the Severn estuary, and the same document also indicates the existence of an intermediate station at Bitton. South of Bath there was an important settlement at Camerton and a smaller one lay on the eastward road at Verlucio (Sandy Lane). In addition to Bath, which he calls Aquae Calidae (Hot Springs), Ptolemy also places a town called Iscalis in this area, but it has not yet been satisfactorily identified.

Villas are very numerous round Bath, and rural temples are known at Pagan's Hill (in the parish of Chew Stoke) and at Nettleton Shrub on the Fosse Way, the latter possibly marking the boundary with the Dobunni. Industry is represented by stone quarries near Bath, ironstone working near Sandy Lane, the manufacture of pewter at Camerton and a pottery at Shepton Mallet. The lead mines of Mendip, centred on Charterhouse, were probably administered extraterritorially; a recent examination by Professor Palmer of a number of lead pigs has led to the conclusion that either Charterhouse or the mining district as a whole bore a name beginning Veb. . . .

The central part of the canton is devoid of towns and nearly so of villas, though evidence of agricultural activity is plentiful, and it has been suggested, as noted above, that part at least of this country was an imperial estate administered from Sorviodunum (Old Sarum); but this, though an important road centre, has so far yielded little information beyond the traces of Roman building buried deep beneath the Norman castle mound and a nucleus of occupation debris outside the hill fort to the east which probably represents a posting station.

The Brigantes inhabited the northern part of the province, extending, so Ptolemy tells us, from sea to sea; that they occupied an exceptionally large area is confirmed by Tacitus' statement that they were the most numerous tribe, for they cannot have been very thick on the ground. Ptolemy attributes nine πόλεις to them—Epiacum (possibly Whitley Castle), Vinnovium (Binchester), Caturactonium (Catterick), Calagum (probably Overborough), Isurium (Aldborough), Rigodunum (possibly Ingleborough), Olicana (possibly Ilkley), Eboracum (York) and Camulodunum (probably Slack). Most of these places were Roman forts, but their names, taken together with dedications to the tribal guardian deity Brigantia from South Shields, Castlesteads and Birrens, suggest that their northern frontier approximated to the line of Hadrian's Wall (which is unhappily overlooked by Ptolemy) with a possible northward extension at its western end. To the east they marched with the Parisi, who occupied an area nearly corresponding with the East Riding of Yorkshire, and on the west lay the Irish Sea. Some doubt, however, attaches to the question of their southern border and this requires further discussion.

The identification of Camulodunum with Slack agrees well with its occurrence in the *Ravenna Cosmography* and, by its juxtaposition to Cambodunum, helps to explain the corruption of the text of the *Antonine Itinerary* in this area. There is little doubt, however, that the name was transferred to the Roman fort from a neighbouring native hill fort, and equally little doubt that the hill fort in question was Castle Hill, Almondbury, near Huddersfield. The attribution of Almondbury to the Brigantes seemed to be confirmed by the discovery, at Honley and allegedly in the hill fort itself, of so-called 'Brigantian' coins, the Honley hoard including a coin which was confidently ascribed to Cartimandua. Mr. Derek Allen's demonstration that the coins in question belong more probably to the Coritani (and that the 'Cartimandua' coin cannot be so read) puts the matter in a new light. Structurally Almondbury has more in common with the hill forts to the south of it, and it has also yielded a scrap of pre-conquest Arretine pottery, which is more

142

likely to have reached it from the south than from the north. Further, a link with the presumed Belgic dynasty who issued the Coritanian coins might explain the reference in the name to the Belgic war god Camulos. Some doubt has already been cast on the reliability of Ptolemy's tribal attributions in border districts, and that the frontier ran near here is in any case suggested by the occurrence in the Calder basin, as on the northern marches, of dedications to the Brigantian tribal deity.

As they were the last of the tribes to be absorbed, so the Brigantes made little progress in romanisation. Being mainly highland country, inhabited by highland people, their territory could not easily be civilised in the Roman fashion, and although here, as further south, the early forts were abandoned, they had to be reinstated in the middle of the second century, apparently after a Brigantian revolt. Pausanias probably refers to this when he says that Antoninus Pius docked the Brigantes of much of their territory because they began an armed incursion into the (unidentified) Genunian region, which was subject to Rome. Later, as we have seen, a number of Sarmatian veterans were settled near Ribchester, on land which had also been Brigantian. In effect, the only part which seems to have remained subject to the *Civitas Brigantum* was the Vale of York with small extensions to the north-east and south-west.

The cantonal capital, Isurium Brigantum (Aldborough), lay on the road from York to Catterick. It was not a very large town and so far it is the only walled site of an unequivocally civil character to have been discovered. North of it, towards Catterick, there was a small roadside settlement or posting station at Healam Bridge, and another to the north-east at Thornton le Street, on the parallel road to the north. South of Isurium there was a settlement of some kind at Tadcaster, the Calcaria of the *Itinerary* and the *Cosmography*, and another settlement, apparently civil, at Adel, near Leeds. Southwest of Tadcaster, along the road to Slack and Manchester, lay Cambodunum. Its identity is not sure, but since it appears in the *Antonine Itinerary* on this road, and since the course of the road almost certainly ran through Cleckheaton, it seems most likely that the settlement located there bore the name. This agrees well enough with the *Itinerary* mileage, but the name also appears in Bede, who says that Paulinus set up his cross '*in Cambodono*', undoubtedly meaning Dewsbury. It is difficult to see how (or why) the road from Tadcaster to Slack should have passed through Dewsbury, and it is more probable that though Dewsbury lay in the territory of Cambodunum it was not its centre (*cf.* the case of Letocetum and Lichfield, discussed under Cornovii).

Villas are few in Brigantian territory, and of a low standard, and the most interesting rural buildings are those at Well, where the baths seems to have formed the centre of a religious site. Both lead and iron were mined in Brigantia, but it is unlikely that the former, at least, contributed anything to the local finances, and it is even uncertain whether the Brigantes benefited from the jet obtained near Whitby.

This completes our account of the *Civitas Brigantum*, but it does not, of course, complete the tale of civil life in the land that was Brigantia. There were towns at Catterick, Corbridge and Carlisle, and *vici* are known or suspected at more than thirty forts in the area— some of them fully as civilised as Isurium Brigantum. But they lay in territory that was heavily garrisoned, where martial law was normal, and although they must have affected the local Brigantes, at least economically, they stood outside the framework of tribal administration and it is unlikely that the *ordo* at Isurium exercised any control over them whatever.

CANTIACI

The name of this tribe appears in Ptolemy as Cantii (with a variant reading Cantici) and in the *Ravenna Cosmography* as Cantiaci. It is obviously related to Cantion, the name for Kent which, judging by the reference to it in Diodorus Siculus, was known to Pytheas. As it is both ethnologically and archaeologically unlikely that the same tribal name persisted here from the fourth century B.C. to Roman times, the district name must be primary, the tribal name secondary. This is borne out by the fact that Caesar mentions no tribe called Cantii but refers instead to 'the people who inhabit Kent' (*ei qui Cantium incolunt*). In these circumstances it is probable that the longer form of the name is correct and the canton itself an artificial creation of the Romans.

Ptolemy attributes three towns to the Cantii—Durovernum,

Londinium and Rutupiae. For reasons given above, the inclusion of Londinium is probably an error, though the canton doubtless included east Surrey as well as Kent; Rutupiae (Richborough) was always predominantly a military station and the main official port of entry to the province. Durovernum Cantiacorum (Canterbury), however, was the cantonal capital, with its own port three miles down the Stour at Fordwich. The only town besides Canterbury known to have been walled is Durobrivae (Rochester), but the *Antonine Itinerary* mentions also Noviomagus (probably Crayford), Vagniacae (probably Springhead) and Durolevum (perhaps Ospringe), all along Watling Street, and a settlement of some kind is known at Maidstone. On the coast the *Itinerary* has Portus Dubris (Dover) and Portus Lemanis (Lympne), and although they later became military stations under the Count of the Saxon Shore they may well have had civil antecedents—Dover perhaps corresponding to the Novus Portus (new, that is, as compared with Richborough) included by Ptolemy in his coastal list. Finally an iron port at Hastings, whether civil or military, had road communications with Kent rather than with Sussex.

Of all these towns only Canterbury has been at all satisfactorily investigated, but at least two *pagi* are discernible, the one centred on the cantonal capital, the other on Rochester. Villas are scarce in the former, very plentiful in the latter, especially in the valleys of the Darenth and the Medway. A temple at Titsey, where the London–Lewes Roman road crosses the North Downs Trackway, may indicate the western limit of the canton, but may equally be associated with the nearby villa.

A number of tile and pottery kilns have been noted in the environs of Canterbury, but the chief industrial areas were around the Upchurch marshes, where pottery was made on a large scale, and in the hinterland of Hastings, where iron was mined. In the latter case, however, the discovery in the workings of tiles bearing the stamp of the British Fleet may indicate that they were administered extraterritorially.

CATUVELLAUNI

As they had been the dominant power in pre-Roman Britain, so in Roman times the *civitas* of the Catuvellauni was one of the most important in the province. Even when they had been stripped of their latest conquests they still occupied a large and fertile tract, bounded on the south by the Thames, on the west by the Cherwell, and extending north into Northamptonshire and east into Cambridgeshire and Essex. Their high degree of romanisation is reflected in the fact that in addition to their capital they could boast eight, perhaps nine, other walled towns, but they were not particularly productive of villas.

The cantonal capital was Verulamium, whose history and status we have already discussed. To the south, along the road to London, lay Sulloniacae (Brockley Hill), the centre of an important pottery industry, while to the north-east there was a roadside settlement at Welwyn. To the north-west, where Watling Street crossed the Icknield Way, was Durocobrivae (Dunstable), whose character remains obscure, and beyond it, at the crossing of the Ouzel, the road station of Magiovinium (Dropshort).

In the western part of the canton lay the twin walled towns of Dorchester and Alchester, the one succeeding an Iron Age site, the other possibly replacing an early fort. Between them, in the Oxford region, lay extensive potteries, while at Woodeaton there was a shrine and rural market near the boundary with the Dobunni. The road connecting Dorchester with Verulamium has not yet been found, but Alchester was joined to the cantonal capital by Akeman Street, with an intermediate station at Fleet Marston, west of Aylesbury.

North of Alchester there was a settlement of uncertain character at Blacklands, King's Sutton, and the walled town of Lactodorum (Towcester). This was the third station up Watling Street from Verulamium, and beyond it again was Bannaventa (Whilton Lodge), whence a spur road led to a metal-working centre at Duston, near Northampton.

North-east of Towcester, another walled town stood at Irchester. This is the least known part of the canton, but it included an iron-working settlement of some importance at Kettering.

North-east of Irchester again, at the extreme northern edge of the canton, lay Durobrivae (Water Newton). This town beside the river Nene succeeded an early fort but must have been, for its size, one of the richest in Britain and, as we have seen, may have become the nucleus of a separate *civitas*. It was the centre of the flourishing Castor potteries and boasted a number of rich suburban villas, including one, in Castor village, whose remains were so extensive that it has sometimes been mistaken for a separate town (fig. 8).

From Durobrivae Ermine Street led south, through a little settlement at Sawtry, to Godmanchester, a small walled town and road centre, possibly to be identified with the Durovigutum of the *Ravenna Cosmography*. From it one road ran south-west to settlements at Sandy and Baldock, while Ermine Street continued south, past a posting station at Wimpole Lodge, to Braughing and ultimately to London. South-east of Godmanchester a third road led to the walled town at Chesterton, probably the Durolipons of the *Antonine Itinerary*, across the Cam from the modern Cambridge, and beyond it, by way of a small settlement at Horseheath, towards Camulodunum. South of Cambridge there was a further walled town at Great Chesterford, the successor of an early military site.

The tribal attribution of the western and southern parts of Essex is uncertain. Even if they had once belonged to the Trinovantes, the distribution of the coins of Tasciovanus shows that at the time of the Roman conquest they had been under Catuvellaunian rule for half a century, and it is not unreasonable to include them for consideration here. In any case they were not of great importance. The only place of note was Caesaromagus (Widford, near Chelmsford), and even this has so far yielded no evidence of town walls. Otherwise there were only posting stations—at Bishop's Stortford, Great Dunmow and Braintree on the road from Braughing to Camulodunum, and Little London (Chigwell) on the road from London to Dunmow—and small settlements at Billericay and Prittlewell.

The chief industries of the canton were the potteries already mentioned at Castor, Brockley Hill and near Oxford, pottery- and tile-making in the area south of Verulamium, and the production of salt on the Essex coast. Though some notable villas existed, they were not numerous in relation to the size of the canton and, apart from those near Castor, they were not concentrated in particular areas. Of rural shrines, in addition to that noted at Woodeaton, there were examples near Great Chesterford and at Harlow, while the existence of two others, as yet undiscovered, is indicated by the finds of dedicatory metal plaques at Barkway (Herts) and Stony Stratford (Bucks).

CORITANI

The territory of the Coritani included the modern counties of Leicestershire, Rutland, Lincolnshire, Nottinghamshire, probably Derbyshire, and perhaps the southern part of the West Riding of Yorkshire (see discussion under Brigantes). They thus lay athwart the first frontier of the Roman province, and a number of early military works have been found here. In addition to the legionary fortress at Lincoln there were forts on the line of the Fosse Way at Margidunum (Castle Hill, Car Colston) and Ad Pontem (East Stoke), and a little in advance of it at Broxtowe. All three of these were later evacuated by the army and the two first were succeeded by important civil settlements, but the north-western part of the territory, bounded by a line drawn from Doncaster to Derby and including the lead-mining district of Lutudarum, is covered by the Pennine chain of forts, and military control of it seems to have continued.

The establishment of the *colonia* at Lincoln cut the canton into two parts, the cantonal capital, Ratae Coritanorum (Leicester), lying in the south-western part. South-west of it, at the intersection of Watling Street and the Fosse Way, there was a small settlement or posting station at Venonae (High Cross), and another at Tripontium (Cave's Inn Farm, Churchover) down Watling Street towards the Catuvellauni. North-west of Venonae, and linked to the capital by a direct road, was the small town of Manduessedum (Mancetter), while the Gartree Road ran south-east from Ratae, by way of a posting station at Medbourne, towards Godmanchester and ultimately Camulodunum.

The main development, however, took place between Leicester and Lincoln. Along the Fosse Way there was a settlement at Vernemetum (Willoughby on the Wolds), a town at Margidunum, and settlements at Ad Pontem and Crococalana (Brough, South Collingham), and on Ermine Street, between Durobrivae and Lincoln, there were small towns at Great Casterton and at Causennae (Ancaster). Further to the east, on King Street and its branch, small settlements or posting stations have been noted at Bourne, Stainfield (Hacconby), Sapperton and Sleaford.

The rural development of this part of the canton was similar to that among the Catuvellauni; villas were not very numerous, but some of them attained a degree of refinement in the fourth century. Industry is represented by small potteries and iron-working. Groups of shrines at Collyweston and Brigstock both lay near the frontier with the Catuvellauni, while the site at Thistleton, north-east of Great Casterton, was also of a predominantly religious character.

The part of the canton beyond Lincoln presents something of a contrast, for urban development was very slight, and it is not impossible that in addition to Segelocum (Littleborough), already mentioned, a great deal of it was attributed to the *colonia*. From Lincoln Ermine Street ran north through posting stations at Owmby and Staniwells (Hibaldstow) to the Humber at Winteringham, and similar sites existed at Ulceby and Burgh-le-Marsh, on the road from Lincoln to the ferry across the Wash, and at Osgodby, on a branch road leading north-east from Owmby. At the same time the ancient Wolds trackway called the High Street continued in use, running south from the Humber at South Ferriby, and on it were situated Caistor and Horncastle. These are the only walled settlements known in this part of the country, but the apparently late date of their walls and their very small size suggest that they were places fortes, possibly connected with a coastal defence system, rather than towns in the normal sense of the word. The coastal site at Mablethorpe was probably no more than a fishing village, but a port may await discovery at Grimsby, while local legends suggest that one may have been engulfed by the sea near Skegness.

The chief industry in this part of the canton was iron-working, centred in the Scunthorpe district, where also there were pottery kilns, and the large and important pottery at Cantley, near Doncaster, should perhaps be included. Villas are very few and the only site of note is that at Horkstow, which included a remarkable mosaic pavement depicting a chariot race.

The Cornovii occupied an area roughly corresponding with the modern counties of Shropshire, Cheshire and Staffordshire. Ptolemy attributes two πόλεις to them, Viroconium (Wroxeter) and Deva (Chester). The latter was the fortress of the Twentieth Legion, and in addition to the considerable *vicus* at Chester itself the neighbouring settlements at Wilderspool, Heronbridge and Ffrith are probably to be connected with it rather than with the *Civitas Cornoviorum*. This is certainly true of Holt (probably the Bovium of the *Antonine Itinerary*), where the legion had its potteries and tile factory.

Viroconium Cornoviorum was the cantonal capital. It probably began as the appendage to an early legionary fortress and despite its great size, and the fact that its status is confirmed by the monumental inscription from the forum, there is as yet little evidence for romanisation in the surrounding countryside. There were, however, a number of minor urban centres in the canton. South of Wroxeter, near the frontier of the Dobunni, lay the small roadside town of Bravonium (Leintwardine). East of the capital, along Watling Street, there was a posting station at Uxacona (Red Hill, near Oakengates), a little town at Pennocrucium (south of Penkridge) and another at Letocetum (Wall), each of them succeeding early military sites. Letocetum was evidently intended as the centre of a *pagus*, if no more, for its public baths, which have recently been re-excavated, were begun on a considerable scale, but, as at Wroxeter itself, the original plan was not completed. That territory was nevertheless attributed to it, however, is suggested by the survival of its name as one element in that of Lichfield, two miles to the north—a possible parallel to the case of Cambodunum, noted under Brigantes.

North of Wroxeter a road ran through the small settlement or posting station of Rutunium (Harcourt Park, at the crossing of the river Roden) to Mediolanum (Whitchurch), whose modern street plan suggests a small walled town. From Whitchurch one road ran north-west by way of a small settlement at Malpas to Chester, while another ran north-east to Middlewich and Condate (Northwich). Other minor settlements, at Chesterton (near Newcastle under

Lyme) and Rocester, lay on the road from Middlewich to the fort
at Littlechester, Derby, which also has a civil settlement.

No rural shrines are known in the canton. For industries, salt
was probably extracted in the vicinity of Northwich and Middlewich, but the copper mines at Llanymynech and the lead mines of
western Shropshire (possibly centred on the extensive site at Linley,
More) are as likely to have been under military as under civil control.

DEMETAE

The Demetae are placed in south-west Wales by Ptolemy, who
attributes to them the πόλις of Maridunum. The name also appears
(as Muridunum) in the *Antonine Itinerary* and undoubtedly refers
to Carmarthen. On general grounds a fort is believed to have stood
here, but its site has not been securely identified and such remains as
have come to light seem to indicate a civil as well as a military
occupation. There may only have been a *vicus* attached to the fort
(as seems also to be the case at Llandovery), but it may have
served as a cantonal capital for the Demetae.

Some degree of romanisation of the surrounding countryside is
attested not only by scattered finds of pottery and coins but also by
the existence of six buildings of Roman construction at Cwm
Brwyn, Trelissey, Aber-Cyfor, Llys Brychan, Ford and Parc-
yr-Eglwys (Eglwyscummin). Of these the buildings at Trelissey and
Parc-yr-Eglwys appear to have been inserted into earthworks of an
Iron Age character, but at Cwm Brwyn the enclosing earthwork is
of a romanising form, while the site at Aber-Cyfor included a tessellated pavement. The degree of civilisation attained, therefore, was
very similar to that reached in Devon and Cornwall and a *Civitas
Demetarum*, similar to the *Civitas Dumnoniorum*, is a real possibility.

DOBUNNI

In pre-Roman times the area occupied by the Dobunni included
Gloucestershire, Worcestershire, parts of Oxfordshire and Wiltshire
and much of Somerset, and the distribution of the coins of their
latest rulers, especially those inscribed BODVOC and CORIO, has
suggested to Mr. D. F. Allen that they may already have split into a

northern and a southern part. This lends additional colour to the idea that they are to be identified with the 'Bodunni' of whom, so Cassius Dio tells us, 'a part' came to terms with Aulus Plautius after the defeat of Togodumnus. They do not, however, appear to have received any preferential treatment from the Roman government. The southern part of their territory was incorporated in the *Civitas Belgarum*; the Severn–Trent frontier drawn by Ostorius Scapula ran through their land, and although Tacitus does not name them they must have been among the tribes who so strongly resented the disarming which accompanied it; and finally a part of their country was taken from them in A.D. 97 to provide for the *colonia* at Gloucester.

Their natural wealth, however—one may suspect especially their sheep pastures—enabled them to improve their lot and they became one of the richest cantons in Britain. With a size of some 230 acres their capital, Corinium Dobunnorum (Cirencester), was the second largest town in the province, becoming perhaps the provincial capital of Britannia Prima. It was, moreover, surrounded by villas which were as wealthy as they were numerous, and it was an important road centre.

From Corinium the Fosse Way ran south-west through a small settlement at White Walls, Easton Grey, to the frontier of the Belgae, perhaps at Nettleton Shrub. To the south-east Ermin Way ran past Cricklade to Wanborough (probably Durocornovium) and so into the territory of the Atrebates. Eastwards Akeman Street led by Asthall and Wilcote, through a considerable group of villas, to the Catuvellaunian boundary on the Cherwell. To the north-east the Fosse Way ran through settlements at Bourton on the Water and Dorn to a little walled town at Chesterton (Warwickshire), beyond which lay the Coritani. Just north of Bourton a branch road led to Alcester, another town that was probably walled, from which one road ran south-eastwards to an industrial settlement at Tiddington and over the Fosse to Lower Lea, Swalcliffe, while another ran west to Droitwich, whose Roman name of Salinae points to a salt industry. South of Droitwich there was another small town on the east bank of the Severn at Worcester.

As we have seen, the inscription on the milestone of Numerian from Kenchester suggests that the writ of the *Civitas Dobunnorum* also ran west of the Severn. This area was separated from Corinium by the *territorium* of the *colonia* at Glevum and Kenchester is likely to have functioned as the centre of a *pagus*. That it achieved a higher rank after the reign of Numerian (A.D. 283–4) is improbable, both because of its small size and because of the low degree of romanisation attained in the surrounding countryside. Apart from Ariconium (Weston under Penyard), which was the centre of the iron mines of the Forest of Dean, the only other settlements known—Stretton Grandison, Blackwardine and possibly Hereford—were little more than posting stations, and the general level of life was probably that represented at Sutton Walls, where a small community continued to occupy the Iron Age hill fort.

In addition to iron and salt, which have already been mentioned, industry is represented by a brick and tile factory at Leigh, near Malvern, and by pottery kilns in the same district. The possible examples of border shrines at Nettleton Shrub, Frilford and Woodeaton have already been noted under Belgae, Atrebates and Catuvellauni respectively. A small temple on a *podium* has been identified at Chedworth, where it was probably associated with the villa (*cf.* Titsey, under Cantiaci), and the enigmatic site at Wycomb (Andoversford) may have had a religious basis. The most interesting manifestation of rural religion, however, is at Lydney, in the western part of the canton, where the fourth-century shrine of Nodens, consisting of a temple, baths and guest house built inside an Iron Age hill fort, was evidently an important centre of pilgrimage.

DUMNONII

The Dumnonii inhabited the south-western peninsula of Britain, the modern counties of Cornwall and Devon, with a small part of Somerset, and their name appears in Dumnonium Promontorium, the name given by Ptolemy to the Lizard. Though they did not strike their own coins, the distribution of their characteristic pottery indicates that they extended as far to the north-east as the Glastonbury marshes and had a common boundary with the Dobunni, with whom they were at least partly related. In Roman times the canton of the Belgae was thrust between them, but Ptolemy's ascription to them of the πόλις Uxella, evidently to be connected with the river to which he gives the same name, suggests that the country as far as the Somerset Axe was still attributed to the Dumnonii.

In their territory romanisation seems to have made little progress. The only substantial town was the cantonal capital Isca Dumnoniorum (Exeter), which was connected by road as well as by river with a settlement at Topsham, possibly of military origin. To the north-east an ill-defined settlement existed at Taunton, and the elusive town of Moridunum (discussed under Durotriges) may have been theirs. West of the Exe, the Iron Age port at Mount Batten continued in use and there are traces of settlement on the north side of the harbour, in Plymouth itself. The recently discovered Roman earthwork at North Tawton may be military, but as it is laid out beside and parallel to the road, and so was evidently constructed later than it, it may have been a tax-collecting station, in which case Lady Fox's suggestion that it is the Nemetostatio of the *Ravenna Cosmography* is probably correct. Further west still, a place of some importance lies buried under the sand near St. Enodoc's Church, across the Camel estuary from Padstow, in an ideal position for the western equivalent of a Saxon Shore fort. Though occupation persisted at sites like Trevelgue Head and Chysauster, it was of a native, rather than a romanised, character.

On the other hand Ptolemy ascribes three πόλεις to the Dumnonii besides Isca—Uxella, Voliba and Tamara. Of these Voliba does not appear elsewhere (its identification with Golden, near Probus in Cornwall, is fanciful), but both Uxella and Tamara recur in the *Ravenna Cosmography*. The former, as already noted, must be associated with the Somerset Axe, and the latter must be on the river Tamar. If we accept the identification of North Tawton with Nemetostatio, which precedes Tamara in the list, Tamara should lie in the Launceston area, with the next name, Purocoronavis (?=Durocornavium), representing a Cornish hill fort such as Carn Brea.

If we except the east Devon villas at Uplyme and Holcombe, which probably belonged to the Durotriges, the only romanised house known outside Exeter and Topsham is that at Magor Farm, Illogan, not far from Camborne. Economically the most important product of the Dumnonii was tin, which was extensively mined in Cornwall, and probably on Dartmoor too. Little is known, however, of the organisation of the industry, though a square enclosure at Nan-stallon, near Bodmin, appears to have been associated with the Boscarne workings nearby.

The Durotriges (possibly Durotroges or Durotrages) are shown by the distribution of their pre-Roman coins to have inhabited Dorset, south Somerset, south Wiltshire and south-west Hampshire, and they probably extended also into east Devon. Ptolemy attributes only one πόλις to them, Dunium. This name, which suggests a hill fort, does not occur in any of the later authorities and has been thought to refer to Maiden Castle, but since Ptolemy normally lists only Roman or romanised places it might perhaps be better applied to the early Roman fort built inside the native stronghold at Hod Hill.

The largest town was Durnovaria or Durnonovaria (Dorchester) and this, though listed without a tribal suffix in the *Antonine Itinerary* and omitted from the *Ravenna Cosmography*, was pre-sumably the cantonal capital. It did not, however, stand alone, as Mr. C. E. Stevens has demonstrated. Two of the inscriptions relating to the Severan reconstruction of Hadrian's Wall com-memorate work done by the *Durotroges* or *Durotrages Lindinienses*, who evidently formed a separate *civitas*. The only known walled town in Durotrigan territory apart from Dorchester is Ilchester, whose position in any case invites the application of the name Lindinis in the *Ravenna Cosmography*. Thus the Durotriges, politically as well as geographically, must have been divided, at any rate by the beginning of the third century, into two parts, the one centred on Dorchester, the other on Ilchester.

The south-eastern part, though containing the larger town, seems to have been agriculturally the less prosperous. In it there were small posting stations at Woodyates, near the frontier with the Belgae, and at Vindocladia, beside Badbury Rings, but neither grew into anything resembling a town. From Badbury a road ran south to Hamworthy, on Poole Harbour, where there was a small port, and Dorchester probably had its own port at Radipole, near Weymouth. A settlement of unknown extent preceded the Saxon town of Wareham. There were several small potteries around Poole Harbour, and another at Bagber, near Sturminster Newton, but the most important industry was the extraction and working up of the Kimmeridge shale found on the south coast. Villas are comparatively rare, though a few large houses are known, notably that at Frampton, possibly the family seat of the decurion who gave Dorchester its aqueduct, which begins nearby. Rural temples are known at Jordon Hill, near Weymouth, and inside the ancient fortifications of Maiden Castle.

By contrast Ilchester, though in no way comparable with Dorchester as a town, was surrounded by one of the largest and richest concentrations of villas in the country, while industry is represented by the quarries at Ham Hill, whose stone was extensively used in Roman times. The boundary between the two *civitates* is not known, but the recently discovered shrine at South Brewham, north-west of Ilchester, may mark the border with the Belgae. A shrine of Mars Rigisamus appears to have existed at West Coker.

In addition to Lindinis, the *Ravenna Cosmography* lists a number of other places which should lie in these parts, but only one of them appears in the other authorities. This is Moridunum, which is placed by both the *Antonine Itinerary* and the *Peutinger Table* at fifteen miles from Exeter and so should be near Honiton. Its precise location, however, and whether it should be ascribed to the Durotriges or to the Dumnonii, are alike unknown.

ICENI

The Iceni inhabited Norfolk and north-west Suffolk, and are perhaps to be identified with the 'Cenimagni' who came to terms with Caesar. They took no part in the resistance to the Claudian invasion and were recognised by Claudius as a client kingdom. The relationship, however, was an uneasy one. When Ostorius Scapula drew his Trent–Severn frontier, in about A.D. 47, the Iceni led the resistance to the disarmament which was its corollary and in 60 the revolt of Boudicca brought the full fury of Rome upon their heads. It is, therefore, not surprising that by comparison with other cantons the degree of romanisation attained by them was low.

The cantonal capital, Venta Icenorum (Caister St. Edmunds), was small, and apart from political considerations it lacked the advantages of the later city of Norwich in not being sited on the river. Instead, it was served by a seaport, itself walled, at Caister by Yarmouth. In the south-west part of the canton a settlement at Ixworth succeeded an early fort. Apart from these places all the settlements so far discovered were small—Toftrees, near Dunton, in the north, Woodcock Hall and Brettenham on the Peddar's Way, Snettisham and Narford on the Icknield Way, and Wilton, on the Little Ouse. It is probable that a further site still awaits discovery in the neighbourhood of Icklingham, whose position invites identification with Camboritum, the station named in the *Antonine Itinerary* between Icinos (=Venta Icenorum) and Durolipons (Cambridge).

In the countryside romanisation was most developed in west Norfolk, along the line of the Icknield Way, but even here only two establishments, those at Grimston and Gayton Thorpe, qualify for the title of villa in the restricted sense suggested in chapter 5. In the south the most interesting site is Stanton Chair, three miles north of Ixworth, where the combination of great size with austerity in its appointments suggests that here we may have the centre of one of those estates bequeathed to Nero by Prasutagus.

So far as is known, industry is represented only by potteries, of which the most important were at Hevingham in the north and West Stow and Wattisfield in the south.

PARISI

The Parisi are placed by Ptolemy in an area roughly corresponding with the East Riding of Yorkshire and this, as we have seen, is confirmed by the concentration here of Iron Age chariot burials resembling those found in the territory of the Parisii of Gaul. The only πόλις ascribed to the tribe by Ptolemy is Petuaria (Brough on Humber). Petuaria was a Roman foundation, beginning with a brief military phase, but its name, meaning 'Fourth' in Celtic, suggests that the tribe was divided into four parts and that the Roman town succeeded a pre-Roman centre somewhere in the vicinity, perhaps that at North Ferriby. As already noted, its status was that of a *vicus*, and we have no evidence for a tribal *ordo* of the Parisi as a whole. Of the other three centres, one must surely have been Norton, where a considerable settlement lay adjacent to, but separate from, the Roman fort of Derventio (which had its own *vicus*). A second might be the settlement at Millington (possibly Delgovicia), which included a temple but whose situation precludes any possibility of large extent. It is possible that the other centre was originally Eburacum, but since Ptolemy attributes this to the Brigantes, not the Parisi, this is unlikely.

The romanisation of the Parisian countryside, such as it was, came late, and although Rudston, for example, must be classed as a villa the astonishing naiveté of its mosaics is a useful check on the picture of sophistication suggested by the existence of a theatre at Brough. The most important industry was pottery-making, well represented at Norton, Crambeck, East Knapton and Throlam.

REGNENSES

This canton appears to take its name from the *Regnum*, or kingdom, of Cogidubnus, who ruled over it in the early years of the Roman occupation. Tacitus observes that he remained loyal until his own time, while from an inscription, in which he appears with the citizen's name of Tiberius Claudius Cogidubnus, we learn that he bore the title not only of *Rex* but also of *Legatus Augusti*—an unusual distinction for a client king and presumably conferred for some signal service. His antecedents, however, are quite unknown. Although his capital lay in what had been Atrebatic territory, there is nothing to connect him with Verica, the last of the Commian line, and it is perhaps significant that the reconstituted *Civitas Atrebatum* was not included in his kingdom. Tacitus' statement that after the conquest '*quaedam civitates Cogidubno regi donatae*' could mean either that 'certain states were bestowed on king Cogidubnus' or that 'certain states were bestowed on Cogidubnus to be king over them'. In either case it is clear that the people involved were *dediticii*, at the disposal of Rome, but if the latter interpretation is correct he might conceivably be connected with the Dobunni (given by Dio Cassius as 'Bodunni'), who were the first to make their peace with the invader.

Equally conjectural is the identity of the '*civitates*' he ruled. No coins of Cogidubnus have been found—unless indeed the two silver pieces inscribed CRAB (?=Cogidubnus Rex Atrebatum Britannorum), found the one at Hod Hill the other at Portsmouth, are his. But three distinct areas, which might in A.D. 43 be called *civitates*, can with some probability be included in the *Regnum*. The first is the belgicised area of west Sussex in which lay his capital, Noviomagus Regnensium (Chichester); the second is east Sussex where, as we have seen, the folk of the Wealden Culture had largely resisted Belgic influence; the third is central Surrey, where both the known feeder roads, from Ashtead and from Farley Heath, converge on Stane Street southwards towards Sussex, not northwards towards London. The idea that Cogidubnus' suzerainty extended over other tribes, though attractive as an explanation of the title of *Legatus*, is not yet supported by evidence.

Apart from Chichester itself the canton is very poorly provided with urban centres. The prehistoric site at Selsey, whose dignity Chichester usurped, dragged on an existence of some kind, but as it is now washed away by the sea its story will never be known. To the north, posting stations have been identified at Iping, on the road to Silchester, and at Hardham and Alfoldean on Stane Street; while at Ewell, also on Stane Street, there was a small settlement evidently associated with the springs of the Hogsmill River. In the east the large cemetery at Hassocks should indicate a centre of some kind, though it has not yet been discovered, nor has any trace been found of a civil phase antedating the Saxon Shore fort at Anderita (Pevensey).

Industry is represented chiefly by the iron workings in the Sussex Weald, but a brick and tile factory flourished at Ashtead, in Surrey, in the second century. Villas are distributed mainly along the sea plain of Sussex, often with dependent farms on the Downs behind them, but there is also a notable group along the North Downs Trackway in Surrey and a third group, in the region of Pulborough and Hardham, includes the very large houses at Borough Farm and Bignor. The villa at Fishbourne, just west of Chichester, is remarkable alike for its size and its early development, evidently the result of unusual circumstances. Rural shrines are known at Farley Heath in Surrey and at Chanctonbury Ring and Lancing in Sussex.

The Silures inhabited Glamorgan, Monmouthshire and south Brecknockshire, and they are unique in that we have a specific account of their physical appearance. Tacitus says that their faces were *colorati* (ruddy or swarthy) and their hair usually curly, and he suggests that they must have migrated from Spain. In support of this idea he adduces the persistent belief of the ancients (perhaps derived from a misunderstanding of Pytheas) that the two countries lay opposite one another, but in view of their south-western connections, noted in chapter 2, he may not be far wide of the mark.

Both their status as a *civitas* and the location of their capital, Venta Silurum, at Caerwent are confirmed by an inscription set up by decree of the *Ordo Reipublicae Civitatis Silurum*. Venta was a small town, however, and apart from it there is little to show of civilised life in the canton. The only πόλις ascribed to the Silures by Ptolemy is Bullaeum, evidently to be identified with the Burrium of the *Antonine Itinerary* (Usk), which was a Roman fort. A settlement existed at Redwick, on the Severn estuary south-west of Caerwent, and another, associated with lead mines, at Machen, but both of these are more likely to have had military than civil connections, while Monmouth, the Blestium of the *Itinerary*, was probably a fort. Indeed in this part of the country the military rather than the civil arm was the more important cultural influence and the *vici* attached to forts, such as that at Cardiff, played an important role. As in the case of the Brigantes, nothing is known of their relationship to the tribal *civitas*, but there is hope that something may emerge from the excavation of the very large settlement attached to the legionary fortress at Isca (Caerleon), on which Dr. Nash-Williams was engaged at the time of his death.

A few romanised farms are grouped round Venta, and there were villas at Ely, near Cardiff, and at Llantwit, further to the west; while the existence of another, surprisingly situated at Llanfrynach, near Brecon, is indicated by the discovery there of a large bath house with elaborate fish mosaics.

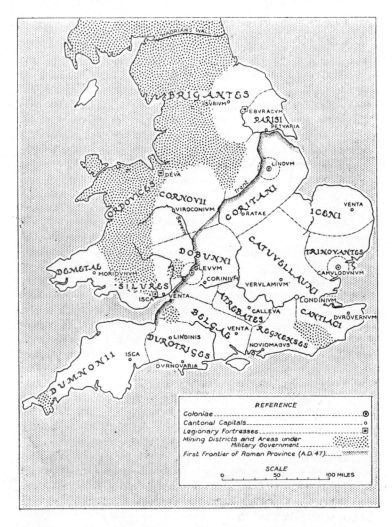

FIG. 9. Political map of Roman Britain. The tribal boundaries are
largely hypothetical (see chapter 6)

6

The Trinovantes, in Caesar's day the most powerful tribe of south-east Britain, had by the time of the Claudian conquest long been vassals of the Catuvellauni. Their reappearance in Tacitus shows that under Roman rule their separate identity was recognised, but they joined the Iceni in their revolt and, like them, paid the penalty for it. The size of their territory and their administrative organisation are alike obscure. The only place ascribed to them by Ptolemy is Camulodunum, and since this was early refounded as a Roman colony the reference does not help, except to indicate Suffolk and eastern Essex as their country; how far they extended into central Essex is not known, and this area has already been dealt with under Catuvellauni.

As to their administrative centre, a number of conjectures may be made. If they included central Essex, Caesaromagus (Widford, near Chelmsford) would be a possible capital, and Mr. C. E. Stevens draws support for this idea from its name. Secondly, the administration may still have been conducted from Camulodunum, whether or not the tribe's territory was attributed to the *colonia* after its refoundation. Thirdly, Combretovium (Baylham House, Coddenham) was an important road centre and well situated to fill the part. Finally, the place called Sitomagus in the *Antonine Itinerary* and Sinomagus in the *Peutinger Table*, apparently near Dunwich and presumably now engulfed by the sea, is also a possibility. The fact that no place is listed with a tribal suffix in any of the authorities does not prove that there was no tribal capital, as the case of Durnovaria may remind us.

Apart from the places already mentioned, the communal settlements in the canton were small and little more than posting stations —Kelvedon (possibly the Canonium of the *Antonine Itinerary* and the *Peutinger Table*, though the name may apply to Rivenhall), Long Melford, at a road junction north-west of Camulodunum, and Stoke Ash and Scole (probably the Villa Faustini of the *Itinerary*) along the road northward from Camulodunum towards the Iceni. Except for a small group near Camulodunum and one isolated example near Ipswich, villas are lacking, and industry is represented only by a few kilns and by salt-boiling on the coast. There was a

162

notable religious site at Gosbeck's Farm, near Colchester, which is
certainly to be related to the local Britons rather than to the Roman
colonists, but whether specifically to the Trinovantes is not so clear.

BIBLIOGRAPHY

On the possible multiplication of *civitates*: C. E. Stevens: 'Gildas and the
Civitates of Britain' (*English Historical Review*, LII, 1937).
On provincial boundaries: J. C. Mann: 'The Administration of Roman
Britain' (*Antiquity*, XXXV, 1961).
On the significance of milestone measurements: Th. Mommsen in *Corpus
Inscriptionum Latinarum*, VIII (ii), 1881, p. 859.
On boundary shrines: C. E. Stevens: 'The Frilford Site—A Postscript'
(*Oxoniensia*, V, 1940).

In the following list only the main references are included; as stated
in chapter 1, it is usually profitable to check entries in the Victoria County
Histories and similar collections against their sources. Occasionally the
identification of a place as a 'settlement' or 'posting station' depends as
much on the finds of burials, coins, etc., made in its vicinity, and on its
relationship to the road system, as on the known remains from the site
itself. It is obviously not possible to cover such cases completely here, but
the local distribution of finds can normally be built up by reference to the
general works cited in each section, while the wider picture is given by the
Ordnance Survey Map of Roman Britain.

LONDON

Royal Commission on Historical Monuments: *London*. III (*Roman London*),
1928.
W. F. Grimes: 'Excavations in the City of London', in Bruce-Mitford
(ed.): *Recent Archaeological Excavations in Britain* (Routledge, 1956).
K. M. Kenyon: 'Excavations in Southwark' (*Surrey Archaeological
Society Research Papers* No. 5, 1959).

COLONIAE

General: I. A. Richmond: 'The Four Coloniae of Roman Britain', in
Archaeological Journal, CIII, 1946.
Camulodunum: C. F. C. Hawkes and M. R. Hull: 'Camulodunum',
M. R. Hull: 'Roman Colchester', and M. R. Hull: 'The Roman
Potters' Kilns of Colchester' (*Society of Antiquaries Research Reports*,
XIV, XX and XXI, 1947, 1958 and 1963).
Lindum: I. A. Richmond: 'The Roman City of Lincoln', in *Archae-
ological Journal*, CIII, 1946. F. H. Thompson: 'Roman Lincoln, 1953',
in *Journal of Roman Studies*, XLVI, 1956, and 'The Roman Aqueduct
at Lincoln' (*Archaeological Journal*, CXI, 1954).

6*

Glevum: H. E. O'Neil in *Trans. Bristol and Glos Archaeological Society*, LXXVII, 1958, and LXXXI, 1962. E. M. Clifford: 'Stamped Tiles found in Gloucestershire', in *Journal of Roman Studies*, XLV, 1955.

Eburacum: Royal Commission on Historical Monuments: *Roman York* (H.M.S.O., 1962).

ATREBATES

General: V.C.H. Berks, I, 1906.

  V.C.H. Hants, I, 1900.

  V.C.H. Surrey, IV, 1912.

  V.C.H. Wilts, I (i), 1957, and I (ii), forthcoming.

  H. Peake: *Archaeology of Berkshire* (Methuen, 1931).

  D. C. Whimster: *Archaeology of Surrey* (Methuen, 1931).

  Berkshire Archaeological Journal, passim.

  Trans. Newbury and District Field Club, passim.

  Surrey Archaeological Collections, passim.

  Wiltshire Archaeological Magazine, passim.

  Procs. Hants Field Club and Archaeological Society, passim.

Silchester: G. C. Boon: *Roman Silchester* (Max Parrish, 1957).

Mildenhall: M. E. Cunnington in *Wilts Archaeological Mag.*, XLV, 1930–2, p. 197. J. K. St. Joseph in *Journal of Roman Studies*, XLIII, 1953, p. 90. *Wilts Archaeological Mag.*, LVI, 1955–6, LVII, 1957–8, pp. 233 and 297, LVIII, 1958–63, p. 245.

Reading: H. Peake: *Archaeology of Berks*, p. 221.

Speen: H. Peake: *Archaeology of Berks*, p. 221.

Thatcham: W. E. Harris in *Trans. Newbury and District Field Club*, VII, 1934–7.

BELGAE

General: V.C.H. Hants, I, 1900.

  V.C.H. Somerset, I, 1906.

  V.C.H. Wilts, I (i), 1957, and I (ii), forthcoming.

  D. P. Dobson: *Archaeology of Somerset* (Methuen, 1931).

  Procs. Hants Field Club and Archaeological Society, passim.

  Procs. Isle of Wight Natural History and Archaeological Society, passim.

  Procs. Somerset Archaeological and Natural History Society, passim.

  Wiltshire Archaeological Magazine, passim.

  Trans. Bristol and Gloucestershire Archaeological Society, passim.

  Procs. Bath Natural History and Antiquarian Field Club, passim.

  Procs. University of Bristol Spelaeological Society, passim.

Winchester: V.C.H. *Hants,* I, p. 285. F. Cottrill in *Procs. Hants Field Club and Archaeological Soc.,* XVIII, 1954, p. 62. M. A. Benet-Clark, ibid, p. 315. S. Butcher in *Procs. Hants Field Club and Archaeological Soc.,* XIX, 1955, p. 1. *Journal of Roman Studies,* XLIX, 1959, p. 131, LI, p. 189, LII, p. 185, LIII, 1963, p. 150.

Bath: V.C.H. *Somerset,* I, p. 219. I. A. Richmond and J. M. C. Toynbee: 'The Temple of Sulis-Minerva at Bath', in *Journal of Roman Studies,* XLV, 1955.

Bitterne: V.C.H. *Hants,* I, p. 330. D. M. Waterman in *Antiquaries Journal,* XXVII, 1947, p. 152. M. A. Cotton and P. Gathercole: *Excavations at Clausentum 1951–4* (H.M.S.O., 1958).

Camerton: V.C.H. *Somerset,* I, p. 289. W. J. Wedlake: *The Excavations at Camerton,* 1958.

Charterhouse: V.C.H. *Somerset,* I, p. 334. J. W. Gough: *The Mines of Mendip* (O.U.P., 1930). On name, L. S. Palmer, H. W. W. Ashworth and R. P. Wright in *Procs. Somerset Archaeological and Nat. Hist. Soc.,* CI and CII, 1958.

Nursling: V.C.H. *Hants,* I, p. 311. O. G. S. Crawford: *Short History of Nursling* (privately, Winchester, 1948).

Old Sarum: J. F. S. Stone and D. J. Algar in *Wilts Archaeological Mag.,* LVI, 1956.

Sandy Lane: M. E. Cunnington in *Wilts Archaeological Mag.,* XLV, 1930–2, p. 180.

Sea Mills: G. C. Boon in *Trans. Bristol and Glos Archaeological Soc.,* LXVI, 1945, and LXVIII, 1949.

BRIGANTES

General: F. and H. W. Elgee: *Archaeology of Yorkshire* (Methuen, 1933).

M. K. Clark: 'Where were the Brigantes?' in *Yorkshire Archaeological Journal,* XXXIV, 1938–9.

I. A. Richmond: 'The Geography of Brigantia', appendix to R. E. M. Wheeler: 'The Stanwick Fortifications' (*Soc. of Antiquaries Research Report,* XVII, 1954).

W. T. Watkin: *Roman Lancashire,* 1883.

Archaeologia Aeliana, passim.

Trans. Cumberland and Westmorland Antiquarian and Archaeological Society, passim.

Trans. Lancashire and Cheshire Antiquarian Society, passim.

Yorkshire Archaeological Journal, passim.

The Bradford Antiquary, passim.

Papers of Halifax Antiquarian Society, passim.

Trans. Hunter Archaeological Society, passim.

Aldborough: H. Ecroyd Smith: *Reliquiae Isurianae,* 1852. J. N. L. Myres in *Yorks Archaeological Journal,* xxxii, 1934–6, p. 229. M. K. Clark in *Yorks Archaeological Journal,* xxxii, 1934–6, p. 459 and xxxiv, 1938–9, pp. 90 and 232. J. N. L. Myres, K. A. Steer and M. K. Chitty in *Yorks Archaeological Journal,* xl, 1959, pp. 1–77.

Adel: M. K. Clark in *Yorks Archaeological Journal,* xxxii, 1934–6, pp. 229 and 459. B. W. J. Kent in *Yorks Archaeological Journal,* xxxiv, 1938–9, p. 231.

Catterick: J. S. Wacher in *Journal of Roman Studies,* l, 1960, p. 217.

Cleckheaton: F. Villy in *Bradford Antiquary,* viii (new series vi), 1940, p. 17.

Healam Bridge: D. M. Waterman in *Yorks Archaeological Journal,* xxxvii, 1948–51, p. 522.

Tadcaster: F. and H. W. Elgee: *Archaeology of Yorkshire,* p. 170. M. K. Clark in *Yorks Archaeological Journal,* xxxiii, 1936–8, p. 219 (reporting the discovery of coffin—'one of the very few Roman finds that have ever been made in or near Tadcaster'. But the -caster name and the evident identity of the place with Calcaria make a settlement of some kind certain).

Thornton le Street: 'Roman Coin, Pottery, etc. found' (O.S. 6-inch, 1913) on line of Roman road.

CANTIACI

General: V.C.H. Kent, iii, 1932.
R. F. Jessup: *Archaeology of Kent* (Methuen, 1930).
Archaeologia Cantiana, passim.

Canterbury: V.C.H. Kent, iii, p. 61. For recent excavations, see interim reports for the Canterbury Excavation Committee by S. S. Frere and F. Jenkins in *Archaeologia Cantiana,* lix, 1946, onwards.

Crayford and Dartford: V.C.H. Kent, iii, p. 88. F. J. C. Spurrell in *Archaeologia Cantiana,* xviii, 1889. For name Noviomagus, A. L. F. Rivet in *Antiquity,* xxx, 1956, p. 44.

Dover: V.C.H. Kent, iii, p. 42. L. Murray Threipland and K. A. Steer in *Archaeologia Cantiana,* lxiv, 1951.

Fordwich (Sturry): F. Jenkins in *Archaeologia Cantiana,* lxii, 1949, p. 145.

Hastings: V.C.H. Sussex, iii, 1935, p. 58.

Lympne: V.C.H. Kent, iii, p. 58.

Maidstone: V.C.H. Kent, iii, p. 98.

Ospringe: V.C.H. Kent, iii, p. 94.

Rochester: V.C.H. Kent, iii, p. 80.

Springhead: V.C.H. Kent, iii, p. 90. W. S. Penn in *Archaeologia Cantiana,* lxv, 1952, lxxii, 1958, lxxiv, 1960, lxxvii, 1963.

CATUVELLAUNI
General: V.C.H. Beds, III, 1908.
   V.C.H. Bucks, III, 1908.
   V.C.H. Essex, III, 1963.
   V.C.H. Herts, IV, 1914.
   V.C.H. Hunts, I, 1926.
   V.C.H. Northants, I, 1902.
   V.C.H. Oxon, I, 1939.
   J. F. Head: *Early Man in South Buckinghamshire* (Wright, Bristol, 1955).
   C. E. Vulliamy: *Archaeology of Middlesex and London* (Methuen, 1930).
   Berks, Bucks and Oxon Archaeological Journal (converted to *Berkshire Archaeological Journal*, 1930), passim.
   Records of Buckinghamshire, passim.
   Procs. Cambridge Antiquarian Society, passim.
   Trans. Cambs and Hunts Archaeological Society, to 1952.
   Trans. Essex Archaeological Society, passim.
   East Herts Archaeological Society Transactions, passim.
   Trans. London and Middlesex Archaeological Society, passim.
   Reports and Papers of the Associated Architectural and Archaeological Societies of Lincs and Northants (to 1936), passim.
   Oxoniensia, passim.
Verulamium: R. E. M. and T. V. Wheeler: 'Verulamium, a Belgic and Two Roman Cities' (*Soc. of Antiquaries Research Report*, XI, 1936). A. W. G. Lowther in *Antiquaries Journal*, XVII, 1937. K. M. Kenyon: 'The Roman Theatre at Verulamium', in *Archaeologia*, LXXXIV, 1935. K. M. Richardson in *Archaeologia*, XC, 1944. S. S. Frere in *Antiquaries Journal*, XXXVI, 1956 (with a note on the forum inscription by R. P. Wright). S. S. Frere in *Antiquaries Journal*, XXXVII, 1957, XXXVIII, 1958, XXXIX, 1959, XL, 1960, XLI, 1961, and XLII, 1962.
Alchester: V.C.H. Oxon, I, p. 281.
Baldock: W. P. Westell and E. S. Applebaum in *Journal of the British Archaeological Association* (new series), XXXVIII, 1932. W. P. Westell in *E. Herts Archaeological Soc. Trans.*, IX, 1934–6, and X, 1937–9.
Billericay: V.C.H Essex, III,.48.
Bishop's Stortford: V.C.H. Herts, IV, p. 150. J. Holmes in *Journal of Roman Studies*, XLVII, 1957, p. 219.
Braintree: V.C.H. Essex, III, p. 155.
Braughing: V.C.H. Herts, IV, p. 150. J. Holmes in *E. Herts Archaeological Soc. Trans.*, XIII, 1954.

Brockley Hill: Royal Commission on Historical Monuments: *Middlesex,* 1937. K. M. Richardson and S. Applebaum in *Trans. London and Middlesex Archaeological Soc.* (new series x = xvi, 1951. P. G. Suggett in *Trans. London and Middlesex Archaeological Soc.* (new series x= xvii, 1952–4.

Cambridge (Chesterton): Royal Commission on Historical Monuments: *Cambridge City,* 1959.

Chelmsford (Widford): V.C.H. Essex, iii, p. 63.

Chigwell (Little London): V.C.H. Essex, iii, p. 88.

Dorchester: V.C.H. Oxon, i, p. 288. S. S. Frere in *Archaeological Journal,* cxix, 1962.

Dropshort (Little Brickhill): V.C.H. Bucks, ii, p. 4. Recent excavations by O. Tapper, unpublished.

Dunstable: V.C.H. Beds, ii, p. 6.

Durobrivae (Castor and Water Newton): E. T. Artis: *The Durobrivae of Antoninus,* 1828, *V.C.H. Hunts,* i, p. 228, *V.C.H. Northants,* i, p. 166. For fort, J. K. St. Joseph in *Journal of Roman Studies,* xliii, 1953. Excavations, *Journal of Roman Studies,* xlviii, 1958, p. 139.

Duston: V.C.H. Northants, i, p. 197.

Fleet Marston: The site lies two miles north-west of Aylesbury and is marked by a heavy scatter of Roman pottery. Discovered by W. T. Millar of the Archaeology Division of the Ordnance Survey while checking the course of Akeman Street. Unpublished.

Godmanchester: V.C.H. Hunts, i, p. 252. C. Hunnybun in *Trans. Cambs and Hunts Archaeological Soc.,* vii, 1952. H. J. M. Green in *Procs. Cambridge Antiquarian Society,* liii, 1960, and liv, 1961, and in *Archaeological News Letter,* vi, 1958, p. 171. *Journal in Roman Studies,* lii, 1962, p. 174.

Great Chesterford: V.C.H. Essex, iii, p. 72.

Great Dunmow: V.C.H. Essex, iii, p. 125.

Horseheath: F. G. Walker in *Procs. Cambridge Antiquarian Soc.,* viii, 1909–10, p. 161. C. E. Parsons in *Procs. Cambridge Antiquarian Soc.,* xxxi, 1931, p. 99.

Irchester: V.C.H. Northants, i, p. 178. *Journal of Roman Studies,* liii, 1963, p. 135.

Kettering: V.C.H. Northants, i, p. 194 (s.v. Weekley).

King's Sutton (Blacklands): V.C.H. Northants, i, p. 201. A. Beesley: *History of Banbury* (1848), i, p. 33.

Prittlewell: V.C.H. Essex, iii, p. 167.

Romford (?Durolitum): V.C.H. Essex, iii, p. 175.

Sandy: V.C.H. Beds, ii, p. 9.

Sawtry: J. R. Garrood in *Antiquaries Journal*, XX, 1940, p. 504, and in *Trans. Cambs and Hunts Archaeological Soc.*, VI, 1947, p. 179.

Towcester: V.C.H. Northants, I, p. 184. J. Alexander in *Journal of Roman Studies*, XLV, 1955, p. 135.

Welwyn: V.C.H. Herts, IV, p. 165.

Whilton Lodge: V.C.H. Northants, I, p. 186.

Wimpole Lodge: W. P. Westell in *E. Herts Archaeological Soc. Trans.*, IX, 1934–6, p. 363.

CORITANI

General: V.C.H. Derby, I, 1905.

    V.C.H. Leics, I, 1907.

    V.C.H. Notts, II, 1910.

    V.C.H. Rutland, I, 1908.

    V.C.H. Warwick, I, 1904.

    C. W. Phillips: 'The Present State of Archaeology in Lincolnshire', in *Archaeological Journal*, XC, 1933 and XCI, 1934.

    H. E. Dudley: *Early Days in North West Lincolnshire* (Caldicott, Scunthorpe, 1949).

    Journal of the Derbyshire Archaeological and Natural History Society (Derby Archaeological Journal), passim.

    Trans. Leicestershire Archaeological Society, passim.

    Reports and Papers of the Associated Architectural and Archaeological Societies (to 1936), passim.

    Reports and Papers of Lincs Architectural and Archaeological Society (from 1936), passim.

    Trans. Thoroton Society of Notts, passim.

    Birmingham Archaeological Society Trans. and Procs., passim.

Leicester: F. Haverfield in *Archaeological Journal*, LXXV, 1918. K. M. Kenyon: 'Excavations at the Jewry Wall Site, Leicester' (*Soc. of Antiquaries Research Report*, XV, 1948). D. T.-D. Clarke in *Trans. Leics Archaeological Soc.*, XXVIII, 1952. R. G. Goodchild in *Trans. Leics Archaeological Soc.*, XXIX, 1953. *Journal of Roman Studies*, LIII, 1963, pp. 133–4 (plan).

Ancaster: C. F. C. Hawkes in *Archaeological Journal*, CIII, 1946, p. 17. C. Green in *Journal of Roman Studies*, XLVII, 1957, p. 210. *Ibid.*, LIII, 1963, p. 131.

Bourne: C. W. Phillips in *Archaeological Journal*, XCI, 1934, p. 160.

Brough (Notts): V.C.H. Notts, II, p. 11. J. K. St. Joseph in *Journal of Roman Studies*, XLIII, 1953, p. 91, and LI, 1961, p. 132.

Burgh le Marsh: C. W. Phillips in *Archaeological Journal*, XCI, 1935, p. 161.

Caistor (Lincs): P. Rahtz in *Antiquaries Journal*, XL, 1960, p. 175.

Castle Hill (Margidunum): V.C.H. Notts, II, p. 15. F. Oswald in *Trans. Thoroton Soc.*, XXXI, 1927.

Cave's Inn Farm: V.C.H. Warwick, I, p. 230. A. J. Pickering in *Trans. Leics Archaeological Soc.*, XVIII, 1934–5, p. 71. *Journal of Roman Studies*, XLIII, 1953, p. 118, and LIII, 1963, p. 134.

East Stoke: V.C.H. Notts, II, p. 34. A. Oswald in *Trans. Thoroton Soc.*, XLII, 1938. J. K. St. Joseph in *Journal of Roman Studies*, XLIII, 1953, p. 91.

Great Casterton: V.C.H. Rutland, I, p. 88. P. Corder (ed.): *The Roman Town and Villa at Great Casterton*, I, II and III (University of Nottingham, 1951, 1954 and 1961). J. K. St. Joseph in *Journal of Roman Studies*, LI, 1961, pp. 119–20.

High Cross: V.C.H. Warwick, I, p. 232. A. J. Pickering in *Trans. Leics Archaeological Soc.*, XVIII, 1934–5, p. 47.

Horncastle: C. F. C. Hawkes in *Archaeological Journal*, CIII, 1946, p. 22.

Littleborough: V.C.H. Notts, II, p. 19.

Mablethorpe: C. W. Phillips in *Archaeological Journal*, XCI, 1934, p. 174.

Mancetter: V.C.H. Warwick, I, p. 233. B. H. St. J. O'Neil in *Birmingham Archaeological Soc. Trans.*, LIII, 1928, p. 173. A. J. Pickering in *Trans. Leics Archaeological Soc.*, XVIII, 1934–5, p. 157. A. Oswald and P. Gathercole in *Birmingham Archaeological Soc. Trans.*, LXXIV, 1958, p. 30.

Medbourne: J. Nichols: *History and Antiquities of Leicestershire*, II (ii), 1798, p. 717. *V.C.H. Leics*, I, p. 214 (but confusing the site of the posting station with that of the villa, which lies south-east of it).

Osgodby: C. W. Phillips in *Archaeological Journal*, XCI, 1934, p. 171 (s.v Kirkby cum Osgodby).

Owmby: C. W. Phillips in *Archaeological Journal*, XCI, 1934, p. 176.

Sapperton: C. W. Phillips in *Archaeological Journal*, XCI, 1934, p. 179.

Scunthorpe: H. E. Dudley: *Early Days in North West Lincs*, chap. XIII and p. 237.

Sleaford: C. W. Phillips in *Archaeological Journal*, XCI, 1934, p. 181.

South Ferriby: C. W. Phillips in *Archaeological Journal*, XCI, 1934, pp. 133 and 166.

Stainfield (Hacconby): C. W. Phillips in *Archaeological Journal*, XCI, 1934, p. 182.

Staniwells (Hibaldstow): C. W. Phillips in *Archaeological Journal*, XCI, 1934, p. 169.

Thistleton: V.C.H. Rutland, I, p. 90. S. A. Butcher in *Journal of Roman Studies*, XLVII, 1957, p. 212. E. Greenfield, *ibid.*, XLVIII, p. 137, XLIX, p. 113, L, p. 224, LI, p. 175 and LII, 1962, p. 172.

Ulceby (by Fordington): C. W. Phillips in *Archaeological Journal*, XCI, 1934, p. 184.

Willoughby on the Wolds: V.C.H. Notts, II, p. 17.

Winteringham: C. W. Phillips in *Archaeological Journal*, XCI, 1934, p. 186.

CORNOVII

General: V.C.H. Hereford, I, 1908.

> *V.C.H. Shropshire*, I, 1908.
>
> *V.C.H. Staffs*, I, 1908
>
> *V.C.H. Warwick*, I, 1904.
>
> I. A. Richmond: 'The Cornovii', in Foster & Alcock (ed.): *Culture and Environment* (Routledge, 1963).
>
> L. F. Chitty: 'An Introduction to Shropshire Archaeology', in *Archaeological Journal*, CXIII, 1956, p. 178.
>
> Ellis Davies: *Prehistoric and Roman Remains of Denbighshire* (Cardiff, 1929) and *Prehistoric and Roman Remains of Flintshire* (Cardiff, 1949).
>
> W. T. Watkin: *Roman Cheshire* (1886).
>
> *Birmingham Archaeological Society Trans. and Procs.*, passim.
>
> *Journal of the Chester and North Wales Architectural, Archaeological and Historic Society*, passim.
>
> *Trans. Lancashire and Cheshire Antiquarian Society*, passim.
>
> *Trans. Shropshire Archaeological Society*, passim.
>
> *North Staffordshire Field Club Trans.*, passim.
>
> *Trans. Woolhope Naturalists Field Club*, passim.

Wroxeter: V.C.H. Salop, I, p. 220. J. P. Bushe-Fox: 'Excavations on the Site of the Roman Town at Wroxeter' (*Soc. of Antiquaries Research Reports*, I, 1913, II, 1914 and IV, 1916). D. Atkinson: *Excavations at Wroxeter 1923–7* (O.U.P., 1942). K. M. Kenyon in *Archaeologia*, LXXXVIII, 1940. J. K. St. Joseph in *Journal of Roman Studies*, XLIII, 1953, pp. 81, 84, 88, and XLV, 1955, p. 88. For current excavations, see notes by G. Webster in *Journal of Roman Studies*, XLIII, 1953, onwards. For aqueduct, G. Webster and D. Hollingsworth in *Trans. Shropshire Archaeological Soc.*, LVI, 1959, p. 133.

Chesterton (Newcastle under Lyme): V.C.H. Staffs, I, p. 189. T. Pape in *North Staffs Field Club Trans.*, LXVIII, 1934, p. 159. J. M. T. Charlton in *North Staffs Journal of Field Studies*, I, 1961, p. 26.

Ffrith: Ellis Davies: *Prehistoric and Roman Remains of Flintshire*, p. 226.

Harcourt Park: The name Rutunium and the *Itinerary* mileages both indicate a site near the Roden. Roman pottery has been found north of the point where the Roman road crosses the river.

Heronbridge: B. R. Hartley and K. F. Kaine in *Journal of the Chester and*

North Wales Architectural, Archaeological and Historic Soc., XLI, 1954.

Holt: W. F. Grimes in *Y Cymmrodor*, XLI, 1930.

Leintwardine: V.C.H. Hereford, I, p. 183. S. C. Stanford in *Trans. Woolhope Nat. Field Club*, XXXVI, 1959, p. 210.

Linley (More): V.C.H. Shropshire, I, p. 257.

Littlechester (Derby): G. Webster in *Derbyshire Archaeological Journal*, LXXXI, 1961, p. 85.

Malpas: W. T. Watkin: *Roman Cheshire*, p. 286.

Middlewich (Kinderton): W. T. Watkin: *Roman Cheshire*, p. 243. D. Atkinson in *Journal of Roman Studies*, XI, 1921, p. 205.

Northwich: W. T. Watkin: *Roman Cheshire*, p. 251.

Penkridge (Stretton): V.C.H. Staffs, I, p. 192. J. K. St. Joseph in *Journal of Roman Studies*, XLIII, 1953, p. 92, and *Birmingham Archaeological Soc. Trans.*, LXXIV, 1958, p. 1.

Red Hill: J. K. St. Joseph in *Journal of Roman Studies*, XLIII, 1953, p. 84.

Rocester: V.C.H. Staffs, I, p. 192. G. Webster in *North Staffs Journal of Field Studies*, II, 1962, p. 37.

Wall: V.C.H. Staffs, I, p. 193. C. Lynam in *North Staffs Field Club Trans.*, XLVII, 1913, p. 139 and XLIX, 1915, p. 132. H. R. Hodgkinson in *Birmingham Archaeological Soc. Trans.*, LII, 1927, p. 308. R. Mott: *Letocetum* (1929). J. K. St. Joseph in *Journal of Roman Studies*, XLIII, 1953, p. 83. G. A. Webster in *Birmingham Archaeological Soc. Trans.*, LXXIV, 1956, p. 12, and LXXV, 1959, p. 24.

Whitchurch: V.C.H. Salop, I, p. 277.

Wilderspool (Warrington): T. May: *Warrington's Roman Remains* (Warrington, 1904).

DEMETAE

General: F. Haverfield: 'Military Aspects of Roman Wales', in *Trans. of the Honourable Society of Cymmrodorion*, 1908–9.

R. E. M. Wheeler: *Prehistoric and Roman Wales* (O.U.P., 1925).

V. E. Nash-Williams: *The Roman Frontier in Wales* (University of Wales Press, 1954).

I. Lloyd: *History of Carmarthenshire*, 1935.

Archaeologia Cambrensis, passim.

Bulletin of the Board of Celtic Studies, passim.

Carmarthen Antiquary, passim.

Carmarthen: V. E. Nash-Williams: *Roman Frontier in Wales*, p. 87. Many finds in Carmarthen Museum.

Llandovery: V. E. Nash-Williams: *Roman Frontier in Wales*, p. 67.

Minor Sites: Aber-Cyfor: J. Lloyd: *History of Carmarthenshire,* I, pp. 105, 108.

> *Cwm Brwyn:* J. Ward in *Archaeologia Cambrensis* (6th series), VII, 1907, pp. 175, 226.

> *Ford:* R. Fenton: *Historical Tour through Pembroke* (1811), p. 331. F. Haverfield in *Trans. Hon. Soc. of Cymmrodorion,* 1908–9, p. 165.

> *Llys Brychan, Llangadog:* M. G. Jarrett in *Carmarthen Antiquary,* IV, 1962, p. 2.

> *Parc-yr-Eglwys:* H. N. Savory in *Bulletin of Board of Celtic Studies,* XVI, 1954, p. 67.

> *Trelissey:* V. E. Nash-Williams: *Roman Frontier in Wales* p. 87 n.

DOBUNNI

General: *V.C.H. Hereford,* I, 1908.

> *V.C.H. Oxon,* I, 1939.

> *V.C.H. Warwick,* I, 1904.

> *V.C.H. Wilts,* I (i), 1957, and I (ii), forthcoming.

> *V.C.H. Worcs,* I, 1901.

> G. B. Witts: *Archaeological Handbook of the County of Gloucestershire* (Cheltenham, 1883).

> R. E. M. Wheeler: 'Roman Herefordshire', in Royal Commission on Historical Monuments: *Herefordshire,* III, 1934, p. xlix.

> D. R. Dudley: 'The Herefordshire Area in the Roman Period', in *Herefordshire* (*Woolhope Naturalists Field Club Centenary Volume,* 1954).

> *Trans. Bristol and Glos Archaeological Society,* passim.

> *Procs. Cotteswold Naturalists Field Club,* passim.

> *Oxoniensia,* passim.

> *Wiltshire Archaeological Magazine,* passim.

> *Trans. Woolhope Naturalists Field Club,* passim.

> *Trans. Worcestershire Archaeological Society,* passim.

> *Birmingham Archaeological Society Trans. and Procs.,* passim.

Cirencester: F. Haverfield: 'Roman Cirencester', in *Archaeologia,* LXIX, 1917–18. D. M. Rennie in *Antiquaries Journal,* XXXVII, 1957, p. 206. J. S. Wacher, reports in *Antiquaries Journal,* XLI, 1961, onwards.

Alcester: *V.C.H. Warwick,* I, p. 236. W. A. Seaby in *Birmingham Archaeological Soc. Trans.,* LXVI, 1946, p. 35. H. V. Hughes, *ibid.,* LXXVI, 1958, p. 10, and LXXVII, 1959, p. 27.

Asthall: *V.C.H. Oxon,* I, p. 330. P. M. M. Cook in *Oxoniensia,* XX, 1955, p. 29.

Blackwardine: V.C.H. Hereford, I, p. 195.

Bourton on the Water : H. E. O'Neil in *Trans. Bristol and Glos Archaeological Soc.*, LVII, 1935, p. 234.

Chesterton (Warwickshire): V.C.H. Warwick, I, p. 234. *Birmingham Archaeological Soc. Trans.*, XLIX, 1923, p. 58. G. Webster in *Journal of Roman Studies*, LII, 1962, p. 171.

Dorn: V.C.H. Worcs, I, p. 221. J. K. St. Joseph in *Journal of Roman Studies*, LI, 1961, p. 132.

Droitwich: V.C.H. Worcs, I, p. 208. H. R. Hodgkinson in *Birmingham Archaeological Soc. Trans.*, LI, 1925–6, p. 35 and LII, 1927, p. 312. J. K. St. Joseph in *Birmingham Archaeological Soc. Trans.*, LXIV, 1941, p. 39. P. Gelling, *ibid.*, LXXV, 1957, p. 1.

Hereford: V.C.H. Hereford, I, p. 192. G. Marshall in *Trans. Woolhope Naturalists Field Club*, 1940, p. 67.

Kenchester: G. H. Jack and A. G. K. Hayter: 'The Romano-British Town of Magna' (*Reports of the Research Committee of the Woolhope Club*, I and II, 1916 and 1926). G. H. Jack and A. G. K. Hayter in *Trans. Woolhope Nat. Field Club*, 1918–19, p. 99. J. K. St. Joseph in *Journal of Roman Studies*, XLIII, 1953, p. 92 and plate xiv. G. A. Webster in *Trans. Woolhope Nat. Field Club*, XXXV, 1956, and *Journal of Roman Studies*, XLVII, p. 211, XLVIII, p. 136, XLIX, p. 111, LI, p. 171, and LII, 1962, p. 169.

Lower Lea, Swalcliffe: V.C.H. Oxon, I, p. 308.

Stretton Grandison: V.C.H. Hereford, I, p. 195.

Tiddington: W. J. Fieldhouse, T. May and F. C. Wellstood: *A Romano-British Industrial Site near Tiddington, Stratford on Avon* (Stratford-upon-Avon, 1931).

Wanborough: M. E. Cunnington in *Wiltshire Archaeological Magazine*, XLV, 1930–2, p. 207. A. D. Passmore: *The Roman Road from Caerleon to Silchester* (Swindon, 1948).

Weston under Penyard: V.C.H. Hereford, I, p. 187. G. H. Jack: 'Excavations on the Site of Ariconium' (*Woolhope Nat. Field Club*, 1923).

White Walls, Easton Grey: M. E. Cunnington in *Wiltshire Archaeological Magazine*, XLV, 1930–2, p. 166.

Wilcote: V.C.H. Oxon, I, p. 344.

Worcester: V.C.H. Worcs, I, p. 203. D. R. Shearer in *Journal of Roman Studies*, LIII, 1963, p. 131.

Wycomb: W. L. Lawrence in *Procs. Society of Antiquaries* (2nd series), II, 1861–4, pp. 302, 351, 422, and III, 1864–7, pp. 129, 396. H. E. O'Neil and A. D. Saunders in *Trans. Bristol & Glos. Archaeological Soc.*, LXXXVIII, 1959, p. 161.

DUMNONII

General: V.C.H. Cornwall, Part 5, 1924.

    V.C.H. Somerset, I, 1906.

    H. O'N. Hencken: *Archaeology of Cornwall and Scilly* (Methuen, 1932).

    D. P. Dobson: *Archaeology of Somerset* (Methuen, 1931).

    Cornish Archaeology, passim.

    Journal of the Royal Institution of Cornwall, passim.

    Trans. of the Devonshire Association, passim.

    Trans. of the Devon Archaeological Exploration Society, passim.

    Procs. Somerset Archaeological and Natural History Society, passim.

Exeter: A. Fox: *Roman Exeter* (Manchester University Press, 1952).

Chysauster: H. O'N. Hencken in *Archaeologia*, LXXXIII, 1933.

Mount Batten: R. Hansford Worth in *Trans. Plymouth Institution*, XVII, 1932, p. 229, and XVIII, 1936–43.

North Tawton: A. L. F. Rivet in *Journal of Roman Studies*, XLIII, 1953, p. 124.

Rock (St. Enodoc): V.C.H. Cornwall, Part 5, p. 6.

Taunton: V.C.H. Somerset, I, p. 367.

Topsham: L. A. D. Montague in *Trans. Devon Archaeological Exploration Soc.*, II, 1932–6, p. 200. P. Morris, L. A. D. Montague and R. G. Goodchild in *Trans. Devon Archaeological Exploration Soc.*, III, 1937, pp. 4 and 67. A. H. Shorter in *Procs. Devon Archaeological Exploration Soc.*, IV, 1948, p. 20.

Tregear (Nanstallon): V.C.H. Cornwall, Part 5, p. 4.

DUROTRIGES

General: V.C.H. Somerset, I, 1906.

    V.C.H. Wilts, I (i), 1957, and I (ii), forthcoming.

    D. P. Dobson: *Archaeology of Somerset* (Methuen, 1931).

    W. G. Boswell-Stone: *Prehistoric and Roman Remains in West Dorset*, 1893.

    Ordnance Survey Map of Roman Britain, 3rd edn., 1956, fig. 5.

    Trans. of the Devonshire Association, passim.

    Trans. of the Devon Archaeological Excavation Society, passim.

    Procs. of the Dorset Natural History and Archaeological Society, passim.

    Procs. of the Somerset Archaeological and Natural History Society, passim.

    Wiltshire Archaeological Magazine, passim.

Dorchester : C. D. Drew and K. C. Selby in *Procs. Dorset Nat. Hist. and Archaeological Soc.*, LIX, 1937, p. 1 and LX, 1938, p. 51. R. A. H. Farrar in *Procs. Dorset Nat. Hist. and Archaeological Soc.*, LXXI, 1949, p. 63; LXXV, 1953, p. 72; and LXXVII, 1955, p. 128. For amphitheatre (Maumbury Rings), H. St. G. Gray in *Procs. Dorset Nat. Hist. and Archaeological Soc.*, XXIX, 1908, p. 256; XXX, 1909, p. 217; XXXI, 1910, p. 230; XXXIV, 1913, p. 81; and XXXV, 1914, p. 88. For aqueduct, K. M. Richardson in *Antiquaries Journal*, XX, 1940, p. 435.

Badbury: W. G. Wallace in *Procs. Dorset Nat. Hist. and Archaeological Soc.*, LIV, 1932, p. 87.

Hamworthy: H. P. Smith in *Procs. Dorset Nat. Hist. and Archaeologicaȷ Soc.*, LII, 1930, p. 96. R. A. H. Farrar in *Procs. Dorset Nat. Hist. and Archaeological Soc.*, LXXI, 1949, p. 66.

Ilchester: V.C.H. Somerset, I, p. 294. J. Stevens Cox in *Archaeological Journal*, CVII, 1950, p. 94. For name and status, C. E. Stevens in *Procs. Somerset Archaeological and Nat. Hist. Soc.*, XCVI, 1952, p. 188.

Radipole: R. A. H. Farrar in *Procs. Dorset Nat. Hist. and Archaeological Soc.*, LXXII, 1951, p. 94.

Wareham: R. A. H. Farrar in *Procs. Dorset Nat. Hist. and Archaeological Soc.*, LXXVI, 1954, p. 82.

Woodyates: C. F. C. Hawkes and S. Piggott in *Archaeological Journal* CIV, 1947, p. 62.

ICENI

General: V.C.H. Norfolk, I, 1901.

    V.C.H. Suffolk, I, 1911.

    R. Rainbird Clarke: 'Roman Norfolk since Haverfield', in *Norfolk Archaeology*, XXX, 1949–52; *East Anglia* (Thames and Hudson, 1960).

    I. E. Moore: 'Roman Suffolk', in *Procs. Suffolk Institute of Archaeology and Natural History*, XXIV, 1949.

    Norfolk Archaeology, passim.

    Bulletins of the Norfolk Research Committee, passim.

    Reports of Group 7 of the Council for British Archaeology, passim.

    Procs. Suffolk Institute of Archaeology and Natural History, passim.

    Procs. Cambridge Antiquarian Society, passim.

Caister St. Edmunds: V.C.H. Norfolk, I, p. 288. E. A. Kent in *Norfolk Archaeology*, XXIII, 1930, p. 269. Excavations by D. Atkinson, 1929–35, unpublished in full, summarised, with bibliography, by C. F. C. Hawkes in *Archaeological Journal*, CVI, 1949, p. 62. R. R. Clarke in *Norfolk Archaeology*, XXX, p. 146, and in *Journal of Roman Studies*, XLI, 1951, p. 132, and XLVII, 1957, p. 211.

Brettenham: V.C.H. Norfolk, I, p. 314. R. R. Clarke in *Norfolk Archaeology*, XXVI, 1938, p. 123, and XXX, p. 151.

Caister by Yarmouth: V.C.H. Norfolk, I, p. 293. C. Green in *Journal of Roman Studies*, XLII, 1952, p. 96; XLIII, 1953, p. 122; XLIV, 1954, p. 97; and XLV, 1955, p. 136. J. A. Ellison, *ibid.*, LII, 1962, 175–6, and LIII, 1963, p. 137.

Ixworth: V.C.H. Suffolk, I, p. 311. I. E. Moore in *Procs. Suffolk Institute of Archaeology and Nat. Hist.*, XXIV, pp. 167 and 174. D. N. Riley in *Journal of Roman Studies*, XXXV, 1945, p. 82. J. K. St. Joseph in *Journal of Roman Studies*, XLIII, 1953, p. 82.

Narford: V.C.H. Norfolk, I, p. 319. *Norfolk Research Committee Bulletin No. 5*, 1952, p. 2.

Snettisham: R. R. Clarke in *Norfolk Archaeology*, XXX, pp. 151 and 158.

Toftrees (Dunton): H. L. Bradfer-Lawrence in *Norfolk Archaeology*, XXIV, 1930, p. 50.

Wilton: R. R. Clarke in *Norfolk Archaeology*, XXXI, 1955, p. 81, and *Journal of Roman Studies*, XLVII, 1957, p. 211. P. Salway in *Journal of Roman Studies*, LII, 1962, p. 176, and LIII, 1963, p. 138.

Woodcock Hall (Saham Toney): V.C.H. Norfolk, I, p. 321 (s.v. Threxton).

PARISI

General: F. and H. W. Elgee: *Archaeology of Yorkshire* (Methuen, 1933).
Roman Malton and District Reports (Yorks Archaeological Society), I–VII, especially V, M. K. Kitson Clark: 'Gazetteer of Roman Remains in East Yorkshire, 1935'.
Yorkshire Archaeological Journal, passim.
Trans. East Riding Antiquarian Society, passim.

Brough: P. Corder and T. Romans: 'Excavations at Brough on Humber, 1933–7' (*Hull Museum Publications Nos. 182, 185, 189, 194* and *206*). P. Corder and I. A. Richmond: 'Petuaria', in *Journal of the British Archaeological Association* (3rd series), VII, 1942. J. S. Wacher in *Antiquaries Journal*, XL, 1960, p. 58.

Millington: M. K. Kitson Clark: *Gazetteer of Roman Remains in East Yorks*, p. 109.

Norton: M. K. Kitson Clark: *Gazetteer of Roman Remains in East Yorks*, p. 113.

REGNENSES

General: V.C.H. Hants, I, 1900.
V.C.H. Surrey, IV, 1912.
V.C.H. Sussex, III, 1935.
D. C. Whimster: *Archaeology of Surrey* (Methuen, 1931).

E. C. Curwen: *Archaeology of Sussex* (Methuen, 2nd edn., 1954).
Procs. Hants Field Club and Archaeological Soc., passim.
Surrey Archaeological Collections, passim.
Sussex Archaeological Collections, passim.
Sussex Notes and Queries, passim.

Chichester: V.C.H. Sussex, III, p. 9. A. E. Wilson and others in *Sussex Archaeological Collns.*, XC, 1952, p. 164, XCIV, 1956, p. 100, and C, 1962, p. 75, and *Journal of Roman Studies*, XLIII, 1953, p. 125, and LIII, 1963, p. 151.

Alfoldean: V.C.H. Sussex, III, p. 39.

Ewell: V.C.H. Surrey, IV, p. 361. A. W. G. Lowther in *Surrey Archaeological Collns.*, L, 1947, p. 9. *Surrey Archaeological Collns.*, LIII, 1954, p. xxvii.

Hardham: V.C.H. Sussex, III, p. 36.

Hassocks: V.C.H. Sussex, III, p. 57.

Iping: V.C.H. Sussex, III, p. 58. I. D. Margary in *Sussex Archaeological Collns.*, XCI, 1953, p. 1.

Selsey: V.C.H. Sussex, III, p. 65.

SILURES

General: F. Haverfield: 'Military Aspects of Roman Wales', in *Trans. of the Honourable Society of Cymmrodorion*, 1908–9.

R. E. M. Wheeler: *Prehistoric and Roman Wales* (O.U.P., 1925).

V. E. Nash-Williams: *The Roman Frontier in Wales* (University of Wales Press, 1954).

Archaeologia Cambrensis, passim.

Bulletin of the Board of Celtic Studies, passim.

Trans of the Hon. Society of Cymmrodorion, passim.

Y Cymmrodor, passim.

Caerwent: O. Morgan in *Archaeologia*, XXXVI, 1855. T. Ashby, A. T. Martin, A. E. Hudd and F. King in *Archaeologia*, LVII, 1901, to LXII, 1911. A. E. Hudd in *Archaeologia*, LXIV, 1913. V. E. Nash-Williams in *Archaeologia* LXXX, 1930. V. E. Nash-Williams in *Bulletin of the Board of Celtic Studies*, XIV, 1952, p. 242, and XV, 1953, p. 159.

Caerleon (Civil Settlement): V. E. Nash-Williams: *Roman Frontier in Wales*, p. 20, and *Journal of Roman Studies*, XLV, 1955, p. 122. H. N. Savory, *ibid.*, XLVI, 1956, p. 121. G. C. Boon, *ibid.*, XLIX, 1959, p. 102, L, 1960, p. 212 (plan), and LIII, 1963, p. 125. W. J. Davies in *Archaeologia Cambrensis*, CVIII, 1959, p. 133.

Cardiff (Civil Settlement): V. E. Nash-Williams: *Roman Frontier in Wales*, p. 94.

Machen: V. E. Nash-Williams in *Archaeologia Cambrensis*, XCI, 1936, p. 379, and XCIV, 1939, p. 108.

Monmouth: Apart from a few coins no Roman remains have so far been found, but the road pattern and the distances given in the *Antonine Itinerary* clearly indicate that Blestium must have lain at or near Monmouth.

Redwick: V. E. Nash-Williams in *Bulletin of the Board of Celtic Studies,* XIV, 1951, p. 254.

TRINOVANTES

General: V.C.H. Suffolk, I, 1911.

    V.C.H. Essex, III, 1963.

    R. Rainbird Clarke: *East Anglia* (Thames and Hudson, 1960).

    I. E. Moore: 'Roman Suffolk', in *Procs. Suffolk Institute of Archaeology and Natural History,* XXIV, 1949.

    Procs. Suffolk Institute of Archaeology and Natural History, passim.

    Trans. Essex Archaeological Society, passim.

    Annual Reports of the Colchester and Essex Museum, passim.

Baylham House (Coddenham): V.C.H. Suffolk, I, p. 303. S. E. West in *Antiquaries Journal,* XXXVI, 1956, p. 73.

Kelvedon: V.C.H. Essex, III, p. 149.

Long Melford: V.C.H. Suffolk, I, p. 312. N. Smedley in *Procs. Suffolk Institute of Archaeology,* XXVIII, 1961, p. 272.

Rivenhall: V.C.H. Essex, III, p. 171.

Scole: R. R. Clarke in *Norfolk Archaeology,* XXX, 1949–52, p. 151.

Stoke Ash: V.C.H. Suffolk, I, p. 316.

INDICES

The index is divided into four sections, as under:

I INDEX OF ANCIENT PERSONS AND AUTHORITIES

This is further subdivided as follows:

(i) Ancient Authors and Authorities
(ii) British Kings and Queens, with a note of their tribes
(iii) British Peoples and Tribes
(iv) Roman Emperors, in chronological order
(v) Roman *Legati* and *Procuratores* of Britain, in chronological order
(vi) Miscellaneous

II INDEX OF MODERN PERSONS AND AUTHORITIES

Only those mentioned in the text or in the general sections of the bibliographies are listed here.

III GEOGRAPHICAL INDEX

With a few obvious exceptions, places are listed under their modern names, with the Roman names in parenthesis. An alphabetical list of Roman names, with their modern equivalents and a concordance of the authorities for their attribution, will be found on pages 25–7 of the introduction to *The Ordnance Survey Map of Roman Britain* (3rd edn., 1956).

For the names of peoples and tribes, *see* Index I.

IV SUBJECT INDEX

In all sections figures in italics refer to the bibliographies, figures in bold type to the illustrations, which are listed by page number.

I ANCIENT PERSONS AND AUTHORITIES

II MODERN PERSONS AND AUTHORITIES

Aber-cyfor, Carm., 151, *173*
Adel, Yorks., 143, *166*
Africa, modern, 27, *28*, 88, 108–10, 111
Akeman Street, 146, 152
Alcester, Warwicks., 152, *173*
Alchester, Oxon., *85*, 89, 135, 146, *167*
Aldborough, Yorks. (ISURIUM BRIGANTUM), 83, 92, 95, 132, 142, 143, **161**, *166*
Alfoldean, Sussex, 78, *85*, 159, *178*
All Cannings Cross, Wilts., *56*
Almondbury, Yorks. (?CAMULO-DUNUM), 142
Ancaster, Lincs. (CAUSENNAE), 78, *85*, 95, 148, *169*
Andover, Hants (near VINDOMIS), 118, 140–1
Andoversford, Glos. (*see* Wycomb)
Anthée, Belgium, 126
Antonine Wall, 92
Arras, Yorks., 35
Ashtead, Surrey, 125, *128*, 159
Asthall, Oxon., 152, *173*
Atworth, Wilts., 110, *128*
Avon, River, Hants., 133
Axe, River, Somerset (UXELLA), 154

Badbury Rings, Dorset (VINDO-CLADIA), 50, *55*, 76, 118, 155, *176*
Bagber, Dorset, 156
Bagendon, Glos., 46, 48, **49**, *56*
Baldock, Herts., 147, *167*
Bardown, Sussex, 102
Barkway, Herts., 148
Barnwood, Glos., 139
Bath, Somerset (AQUAE SULIS, AQUAE CALIDAE), 51, 84, 126, 132, 141, *165*
Bavai, France (BAGACUM), 96
Baylham House, Suffolk (COM-BRETOVIUM), 162, *179*
BELERIUM, 37
Bignor, Sussex, 112, *129*, 159
Billericay, Essex, 147, *167*

Binchester, Durham (VINOVIA), 131–2, 142
Birrens, Dumfries (BLATOBULGIUM), 142
Bishop's Stortford, Herts., 147, *167*
Bitterne, Hants (CLAUSENTUM), **85**, 96–7, 140, *165*
Bitton, Glos., 141
Blackwardine, Herefords., 153, *173*
Bodiam, Sussex, 102
Boscarne, Cornwall, 155
Bourne, Lincs., 149, *169*
Bourton on the Water, Glos., 152, *174*
Brading, Isle of Wight, **115**, 127, *129*
Braintree, Essex, 147, *167*
Brancaster, Norfolk (BRANO-DUNUM), 95
Braughing, Herts., 46, *56*, 73, 75, 76, 147, *167*
Breckland, The, 47
Bredon Hill, Glos., *55*
Breedon Hill, Leics., *55*
Brettenham, Norfolk, 157, *177*
Brightlingsea, Essex, 138
Brigstock, Northants., 149
Bristol Channel, 35
BRITANNIA INFERIOR, 67, 136
BRITANNIA PRIMA, 67, 136, 152
BRITANNIA SECUNDA, 67
BRITANNIA SUPERIOR, 67, 136
Brittany (ARMORICA), 35, 40, 126
Brockley Hill, Middlesex (SUL-LONIACAE), 146, *168*
Brough, Derbyshire (NAVIO), 134
Brough, Notts. (CROCOCALANA), 148, *169*
Brough on Humber, Yorks. (PETUARIA), 51, 66, 80, *83*, 86, 92, 95, 133, 157–8, **161**, *177*
Broughton, Hants (?BRIGE), 140–1
Broxtowe, Notts., 148
Burgh le Marsh, Lincs., 149, *169*
Bury Walls, Hants, *55*
Buxton, Derbyshire (AQUAE ARNE-METIAE), 84

Caburn, The, Sussex, 50, *55*
Caerhun, Caerns (CANOVIUM), 134